The Runners
A Novella

Christopher Chagnon

Acknowledgments

Tom and Roberta Quarton, Judges Milt and Laura Mack, and Doctor Joseph Braden. Without your conversation and fine wine at the beloved "cabin," this story could not have been told. Thank you.

Also by Christopher Chagnon

The Dregs of Presque Isle

The Ghosts of Presque Isle

The Soldiers of Presque Isle

Copyright © 2018 by Christopher Chagnon
All rights reserved. No part of this publication may be reproduced, distributed, or transmitted in any form or by any means, including photocopying, recording, or other electronic or mechanical methods, without the prior written permission of the publisher, except in the case of brief quotations embodied in critical reviews and certain other noncommercial uses permitted by copyright law.

ISBN-13: 978-1986692410
ISBN-10: 1986692418

This is a work of fiction. Names, characters, businesses, places, events and incidents are either the products of the author's imagination or used in a fictitious manner. Any resemblance to actual persons, living or dead, or actual events is purely coincidental.

Cover design by Cool Shots Inc.

Book design and production by Christopher Chagnon
www.christopherchagnon.com

Published by:
Cool Shots Inc.
5641 County Road 489
Onaway, MI 49765

Chapter One

The cold Detroit River raced beneath the warm, midnight fog, swirling and lapping below the gunwales of the open bow wooden boat, like a thirsty dog's tongue in a bowl of water. Tug Feeney crouched low in the vessel, straining to see, his hand cupped to his ear, listening for other craft on the river. His mates, brothers Mike and Liam O'Meara, did what they could to be small in the boat. They were ten minutes on the water after leaving the secluded shore at Windsor, Ontario. Feeney was in charge, but he was as nervous as the others making the run of twenty-five cases of valuable Canadian whiskey to the east Detroit shoreline. He knew he was expendable, just like the O'Mearas, because they were Irish. He had a sidearm within quick reach, should he need it. Their Jewish bosses cared only about delivery and little about the safety of the bootleg "runners." Each of them would be paid enough to equal a month's wage on the Ford Motor Company assembly line, if they could have found jobs there. Before he'd left that evening, Feeney had told his wife he'd do anything to provide for her and their kids, but he didn't say his job could get him killed.

April, 1929. Prohibition had been in place for nearly ten years. The Jewish and Italian mobs of

Detroit were making money from back-alley stills, bathtub gin, and surreptitious trips across the Canadian border for whiskey. Bootlegged booze was profitable when they cut the product with distilled water. But getting it from Canada to Detroit had its perils.

A low rumble sounded in the fog. "Listen up, I hear something," Feeney whispered to his mates. Before the others could get smaller in the bow, two blasts of a high-powered rifle brightened the river surface for a flashing moment, killing the brothers. Feeney dove to the bow, then rose to his feet, realizing he was unhurt. He raised his empty arms as the approaching boat came into view, continuing its low idle toward Feeney's craft. A burly man, Guido Serrano, stood at the bow of the Chris-Craft, rifle held to his shoulder, aimed at Feeney's head. "Permission to come aboard?" another figure called out, rising from his pilot position. Both men were well dressed, apparently having plans for a social engagement after their work was complete.

Serrano, still aiming his rifle, crooked his head, "Are you frickin' kidding me? Fuck that Mick cocksucker."

"Guido, that's what you're supposed to say, I read it in a book." The Italians laughed, pleased at having intercepted the whiskey shipment for themselves.

They tied the handsome Chris-Craft to Feeney's. Guido stepped onto the smaller boat after dropping an anchor to steady the boats in the fast current. "How about you start loading that whiskey right in here," he said, motioning his rifle at Tug Feeney, then the open bow of his boat. Feeney followed LaPosa's order, keeping his anger inside his tightened chest, and began to off-load the wooden cases. He went about his work slowly, knowing what was to follow once he had all the whiskey stacked in the Chris-Craft.

"Anything you'd like to say, Mick?" Guido said, shouldering the rifle again.

"Yeah, get a message to my wife, tell her I'm sorry...ya' eggplant cunt!"

"What she look like?"

"She'll be the one wearing black at my wake, if you ain't scared to get down to Corktown." Feeney said, still defiant.

"How about I tell her that when I'm pouring this up her ass?" Guido grabbed a handful of his crotch.

"Guido, come on. That's no way to talk to a dead man. Show some respect," LaPosa said.

"You're too, nice." Guido said.

"Fuck yourself, while you're at it! You know Feinstein is gonna' come after you pricks?" Feeney glared.

LaPosa said, "What's he paying you for the run?"

"Twenty," Feeney replied.

"Those two, how much?" LaPosa nodded toward Feeney's men.

"Same."

"I'll see your wife gets the dough. Them, too." LaPosa lit the barrel of a fat, imported cigar.

"That's nice of you, mister. Say, any chance I can come to work for you fellas?" Feeney asked.

"Sorry, Mick, it's been a little slow lately and you got the wrong complexion," LaPosa said. He tapped the ash off the cigar. "Can't blame you for asking, though." LaPosa removed the red rose that was pinned to his lapel and tossed it into the bow of the runner boat once all twenty-five cases had been removed. The rose was his calling card. Carmine LaPosa was an apprentice Italian mobster who was trying to get a foothold in Detroit after breaking away from a New York syndicate to start his own operation without their permission.

LaPosa dragged on his cigar diligently as he and Serrano watched Feeney laboring slowly, purposely, moving the whiskey, occasionally pausing for one of his last breaths. Slowly, the jagged Detroit skyline began to seep through the fog when the last rifle shot diminished to a faint echo. The Chris-Craft powered upstream toward the big city. An hour later, it moored at an east side dock near Grosse Pointe Park. LaPosa ordered three more of his men to carry the cases to an inconspicuous, dilapidated warehouse on shore.

The open-bow "runner" boat was set adrift, left to wander on a downstream path. Two dock workers idled from their morning chores to watch the boat find its place against the rocky shore of Zug Island with three dead Irishmen slumped in its bow.

Several miles away on Hastings Street, near Detroit's Greektown, Ira Feinstein watched his brothers, Joseph, Isadore, and Frank, count cash, placing the bills in neat stacks on a tabletop, last night's haul from the brothels they owned around town. They were dressed in fine, tailored suits and silk shirts, but none of them wore a tie, out of a personal defiance. They called themselves the Purples, a lower east side Jewish gang, operating in an area known as Paradise Valley; their business was racketeering, kidnapping, hijacking, drugs, prostitution, and murder–nearly every crime known to man. Crimes that paid. The powerful Italian mobs of Chicago and New York let them operate in Detroit so long as they helped further their own operations on occasion, as needed. The Feinstein brothers were waiting for word of the shipment of whiskey that should have arrived hours ago.

It was midday. Feeney and his men had failed to deliver the whiskey. Ira knew from past experiences that they must have been intercepted by the police or a rival gang.

Irving Shapiro, a tall, squeaky voiced gang member, bent by a violent temper, hurried into the room highly excited. The Feinsteins counted on Shapiro to carry out any "discipline" when the need arose, like keeping their whores in line. He was a brutal man. Patting his oily forehead with a stained handkerchief, he said, "Our contact downriver said the police found our boat at Zug Island. Feeney and the O'Meara brothers were in it, shot dead. No whiskey, Ira."

Feinstein tilted back in his chair, grasping the wooden armrests where they curved to the chair's seat. "That's three shipments this spring. It's gotta be the Italians. Anything else?"

"Yeah, there was a red rose lying in the bow." Shapiro said.

"LaPosa," Feinstein muttered. "We need to do something about this. I'll call Chicago, talk to Al." Feeling pressure, he undid the top button near his neckline, thinking of the dire consequences that may follow for botching the deal he had with Chicago. Maybe some of them would die because of it? "Smart pool to look into finding a better location to bring our freight over the border? Hear that? I expect you boys to start looking right now."

The room went stale with Ira Feinstein's proclamation, the troubling, unfocused stare that gazed beyond the men. They sensed his immediate concern. So the men set out with the task to find such a place, but it would take some months before they did.

Chapter Two

On October 29, 1929, the stock market collapsed, ushering in the Great Depression. What wealth remained hadn't diminished for some fortunate folks whose money had long been around. Their monetary wells ran deep and were protected. Those who still had it embraced its privileges, and Detroit's remaining wealthy partook and bathed in it glamorously. There still remained automobile tycoons, savvy bankers, shrewd investment men, and corporate CEOs who coddled their successes by renewing private country club memberships and positions within their haughty and decadent societies in the name of culture and defiance to the bleak times. The Detroit Athletic Club, the DAC, was one such establishment that managed to keep most of its members. A posh and very private club, its home was constructed in a Neo-Renaissance style that was ornately adorned, rising six stories above Madison Avenue in the heart of the city's downtown cultural district.

Board members of another private club of lesser stature, the Shoepac Outing Club, met at the DAC to interview a potential new member for inclusion to the remote northern Michigan hunting and fishing club. Some of its members were less fortunate during the culling of the ephemeral wealthy. Ten of the original twenty-five members had resigned due to being broke. The remaining members embarked on finding replacements—a membership drive. Previously, membership was strictly limited to male citizens of the United States who were at least twenty-one years old, and in good standing in some Protestant Evangelical church; soon, however, they would relax such restriction in order to keep the club intact.

Doctor Albert Harrington, who was of the Catholic faith, didn't fit the original membership requirements, but his application was walked through with little interrogation. Present at his interview were J. Henry Linger, a successful piano merchant in Detroit; Anson Parker, a Detroit industrialist; Honorable Milton Mack, a Wayne County probate judge, Delmar Spellman; a noted Detroit photographer whose clients included the city's upper-crust socialites and Bryce Templeton, an importer of exotic specialty woods.

Forty-five-year-old Harrington was the head surgeon at William Beaumont Hospital in Royal Oak. He was an avid outdoorsman who wanted to indoctrinate his sons to the rigors of fishing and hunting in northern Michigan. Anson Parker, the club's president, had been stricken with acute appendicitis that September. Doctor Harrington had performed emergency surgery on Parker, saving his life. Parker felt beholden to the doctor and asked him if he would be interested in joining Shoepac Outing Club, something the doctor had found to be ideal for his sons. Harrington became its newest member in the April of 1930.

Harrington began planning his first trip to northern Michigan immediately, but it wouldn't happen until the snow had melted up north, when the lake's ice gave way to open water, and he could fish.

He set out for his first trip with his two sons late that April. It had taken the Harringtons nearly ten hours of steady driving from Birmingham to reach Rogers City where they switched vehicles.

The Shoepac Club kept a trail beaten Ford Model T in a city parking lot, near Lake Huron, for members to use. It fired up instantly. They began a cross-county, two-track drive to the remote fishing lodge near the south Presque Isle County line where it met Montmorency County.

Anson Parker had warned Harrington of the possible and real dangers of the trip. He'd told them to be mindful of whipping branches that could slap a passenger's face, maybe put an eye out, and countless potholes that could break an axle or flatten a tire. The venerable Model T had dents on dents, showing deep scratches all across its torso. The undaunted wilderness of northern Michigan was where Harrington wanted his boys to meet nature in its uncluttered, unfiltered condition.

There was no telephone or electricity at the lodge–precisely what he was looking for to get his boys away from the poisonous temptations Detroit held. But he knew the rewards of a full creel of brook trout, or smallmouth bass, would outweigh the discomfort of the exhausting trip getting there.

When the trio arrived, the sun was positioned to set within an hour. Ned Vermont, the club's caretaker, was cutting firewood, standing on the push side of a crosscut saw. Ike Powers, his assistant, was on the pull side. Both men wore threadbare flannel shirts and wool pants, with Powers's clothes showing patchwork repair. Both men were from Onaway, too, ten miles north of Shoepac, on Highway 33, a crude road that ran from Atlanta to the south, ending in the small logging and farming town. Vermont lifted his sweat-wet newsboy hat in a terse nod. Powers, showing less physical stress of the event, cast a quick, pleasant look below the brim of his slouching fedora hat, saying "hello" to the Harringtons with his eyes. He walked to the porch carrying an armful of oak firewood and began to stack it outside the cabin entrance. Vermont walked to the Harringtons and extended his square and broad hand to welcome the first-time visitors, introducing himself and his assistant.

"This being your first trip up here, Mr. Powers will teach you the ropes of the place. I apologize for not being able to spend more time with you folks right now, but you see my missus, Anna, she's due any day now, so I've gotta' be close by. She made ham sandwiches for yous; they're in the ice box, along with some Cokes and some milk."

Doctor Harrington had his sons carry their provisions and baggage into the cabin. There wasn't much, but the doctor brought his black medical bag. He thanked Vermont and then switched to more pressing matters. "Any reports on the fishing lately?" he asked.

"Anything with fins are hungry as hobos, right now," Vermont answered.

"That's just splendid, Mr. Vermont." The doctor turned toward his younger son, Tom, who was already assembling his fly rod. "Hear that, son? Hungry as hobos!" His eldest, John, was already inside the cabin snooping about.

"I can't wait, Father. Any place better than another, Mr. Vermont?" Tom asked.

"Oh, I'll leave that up to Mr. Powers, he's the expert. He knows the waters around here better than anyone. What do you think, Ike?"

Powers brushed the sawdust from his forearms, stepped from the porch, and turned to face east where Shoepac Lake appeared dim, dark, and deep. The hues of sunset faintly reached beyond the sloping trail leading to it, but the lake glinted in silver slivers through the tall white pines in the failing evening's light. "Shoepac is deep; I don't know of anyone ever finding the bottom to it. You fellas'll do well on the bass and trout, maybe some pike, but see that smaller lake over there?" He pointed to a lesser lake lying to the west. "That's Lake Francis; it's loaded with big northern pike, especially in the reeds near the shore." Powers had taken notice of Tom's fly rod, and added, "You'll need a bait caster for the pike. There's a few of them inside the cabin. The pike will bite on any spoon, harness, or plug. They're aggressive sons-a." Powers, respectfully, held short of swearing.

Vermont and Powers gave the Harringtons a brief introduction to the cabin, lit lanterns, and made a fire in the woodstove. The spring evenings were still cold, and Vermont said they shouldn't be surprised if it snowed some during the night. There were two canoes docked on Shoepac's shore for the Harringtons to use, but they would have to portage one of them to Lake Francis if they chose to fish there.

Then the caretakers departed the club in Vermont's pickup as darkness deepened the blackness of the forest that surrounded the cabin. They would return the next day to attend to their new guests.

Vermont and Powers had built the cedar log cabin ten years earlier, when the club had first formed. It was Spartan in amenities and size–only twenty feet by twenty-eight feet overall. A screened porch wrapped around the building on three sides, leaving the north side bare and alone. Fifty feet away stood the outhouse with a fresh hole dug a week earlier.

Within the cabin, a pair of well-used bear-paw snow shoes hung from a rusty spike near the doorway. A sixteen-gauge Winchester Model 12 shotgun rested on dowels above the door. A ruffed grouse mount, with wings flared, hung by a thin wire attached to a cedar branch. Horseshoe nails fastened the bird to the chinked wall. Harrington found a row of opened whiskey and vodka bottles concealed by a wide, rough sawn board inside the crude cupboard by means of two angled iron supports, should a game warden stop by for an impromptu inspection. Prohibition was still in effect. A variety of mounted fish of trophy length were displayed throughout the cabin, their top surfaces thickening with ambient dust. The chinking between the logs showed graying from time and a decade of fireplace smoke. Dented aluminum pots and black cast-iron skillets dangled from a crossbeam above a wood cook-stove in the kitchen area of the open-floor design. Four sets of double bunk beds, made of hand-hewn cedar logs with thick mattresses drooping over their edges, butted against the log walls. A single pillow rested on top of the woolen bedrolls that was neatly coiled at the foot of each bed.

It was well past ten o'clock in the evening when Doctor Harrington turned and extinguished the flaming wick back in each lantern before climbing into his bunk. Outside the cabin, the lake's amphibian voices chirped their ancient songs for most of the night.

Morning arrived within a thick haze of fog that soon departed in hesitant swirls from the glass-like surface of Shoepac Lake, leaving a crisp mirror reflecting the forming clouds. Two days earlier the shoreline had been feathered in fragile spring ice, but the present warm spell had returned it to plain water.

Doctor Albert Harrington stood near the canoe holding his fishing gear, waiting for his excited seventeen-year-old son, Tom, to settle in the stern of the craft. When Doctor Harrington pushed off he called out to his older son, John, "Are you sure you don't want to go? They'll be biting like angry Chihuahuas and hungry hobos right now."

Nineteen-year-old John Harrington was studious and of high intelligence. He watched from the elevated precipice where the cedar log cabin stood near the path leading down to the lake. A thick sweater was draped over his shoulders, its sleeves tied across his chest. He held *The Great Gatsby* above his head and waved it. "I'm good with this, just about finished with it. Good luck!" He returned to the lodge where he would read the book in an Adirondack chair inside the porch that overlooked the lake.

John was not enamored with the obligation of having to split kindling wood for the stove or battling the black flies and mosquitoes that were beginning to hoover beyond the screened porch. He was most at ease reading while others, like Tom and his father, preferred the physical motions of the outdoors. He was on spring break from the University of Michigan where he was a sophomore, majoring in philosophy, and was keenly interested in ancient Eastern religion and philosophy–Buddha, in particular. Doctor

Harrington hoped John would have remained in the premedical program after his first year, but his interests changed when he took his first philosophy class. The prospect of waving a fly rod back and forth across the surface of a remote lake failed to interest him, too, but he had reluctantly agreed to go on the trip. Tom Harrington, on the other hand, was as opposite to his brother's nonchalance in these matters as a burning ember is opposed to an icicle. Tom was the ember, while John was the ice. Tom was athletic in his medium frame, standing six feet tall. He was the captain of his high school golf team and had a burning ambition to become accomplished after he enrolled at Michigan State University the following fall. He hadn't discovered what he would be accomplished in, but he was patient. In the meantime, he embraced the concept of exploring the ruggedness of northern Michigan, the anticipation of a fish rising to a fly, and setting out on foot through the damp, alder growth in search of ruffed grouse, experiences he hoped to have after listening to his father's many recollections of such adventures when he was a young man growing up in Michigan's Upper Peninsula.

A sufficient western breeze kept the bugs away on the lake while father and son finessed their looping lines in long, artful casts, placing their flies near the subtle lake's reedy shoreline.

"So how do you suppose Queenie will take to this place?" the doctor asked, knowing beforehand his sixteen-year-old daughter's ambition of becoming a professional singer could stymie any hope of her being interested in the quaintness of the club, preferring her budding socialite camaraderie back in Birmingham. Quine was her real name, but Queenie fit her personality like a custom crown. She was the youngest of the Harrington children. From an early age, she had shown a real talent in singing and dancing, and playing the piano. She also exhibited a propensity and desire for the high life of an entertainer, inspired by the stars of Hollywood and radio fame. Belle Baker, Margaret Young, Marion Harris, and Ruth Etting being her current favorites. She often swung into a perfectly sultry rendition of "I'm Nobody's Baby" at the slightest enticement. But the doctor and his wife, Helen, worried about Queenie's propensity for getting into trouble. Her recalcitrant behavior had caused her to be expelled from every public school she'd attended. So, the Harringtons enrolled her in a strict private school, hoping to bring her in line. That plan was evidently failing, too, though her parents had yet to accept this. Queenie was a sulfur match waiting to burst to flame.

"Like tossing a cat in a bathtub, Father. There's nothing here she could find interest in," Tom said. He thought for a moment. "Now, if there was a piano up here, and an audience, then she may come up."

The doctor smiled. "We'll see. Your mother and I plan on all of us coming up here after your graduation in June."

Tom's line lurched and straightened when a splendid brook trout grabbed his lure and then dove hard to get free. Within a short time, they had four trout, and a large northern pike inside the canoe. The pike had nearly broke Tom's fly rod. The fish would provide more than enough food for a meal that day.

Chapter Three

Ned Vermont drove to Ike Powers's place on the outskirts of Onaway at eight o'clock in the morning. His wife, Anna, sat beside him holding a basket of freshly baked bread on her swollen lap. She was taking the bread to the Harringtons. Her cheeks were flush from pregnancy. Though she was close to full-term, she hadn't gained much weight on her small frame. She wore a dull-brown cotton dress that hung loosely about her fragile body. Most everything about her was simple and plain, as uncomplicated as a pair of work boots. She grimaced occasionally, thumbing the wisps of brown hair back to her temples when the pickup bounced over the rough road. She tried to conceal her pain from Ike. She made small talk to take her mind off her discomfort.

Anna served as the camp cook when one was needed, earning twenty-dollars a month, along with tips. Ned's pay was sixty-five dollars, and Ike earned fifty as his assistant. Ned brought Anna because she was having problems carrying what would be their first child. He hoped Doctor Harrington would have an opinion on her condition, maybe even do a quick exam of Anna if they were lucky. The two of them were in their midforties. She had lost three other pregnancies by miscarriage, and they desperately hoped this one would survive. It wasn't that he didn't trust the town's only physician, Doctor Young, but he had gone away on a medical conference, and wasn't expected back for another four days. She would have to be attended by old Rosie Warner, a midwife of crude, practical experience, should she go into labor.

Ike was waiting near the road when they arrived and got in the bed of the pickup. They drove the forty-five minutes to reach the Shoepac Club, arriving just as the Harringtons were departing the dock with a stringer of fish.

"Good morning, folks, I see you've done well," Vermont said at the sight of their catch. He introduced them to his wife as Anna showed the bread to Doctor Harrington. "So pleased to meet you folks. I'd be happy to cook meals for yous if you want."

Doctor Harrington held Anna's hand and gave it a delicate greeting. "Pleased to meet you, too." The doctor observed Anna for a moment, "How are you feeling, Anna? When is the child due?"

Anna shyly responded, "Doc says any day now. I guess I'm alright, though," she said, lowering her head unconvincingly.

"I understand," Doctor Harrington replied. Changing the subject, he pointed to Tom, who was holding the stringer. "Not bad, I'll say. More than enough for lunch today. I can handle cleaning the trout, but this northern? I've never filleted or deboned one with any success." Harrington laughed. "You'd think a surgeon could handle such a task."

"Ike? What do you say you show the good doctor how it's done?" Vermont said.

"I'd like Tom to learn how. He can show me later," Doctor Harrington said.

Ike nodded. "Bring them over here, Tom. I'll show you how to do it." Tom brought the stringer to a knee-high table built for cleaning fish. Anna filled a pan with cold water from the hand-pump well, and placed the trout in the water. She doused the fish with coarse table salt to help remove their slime coating. The pike was still alive, so Ike took the lead pipe that was setting on the table and gave it a swift thud on its head. "First thing you should do before cleaning a pike. They can grab a guy's hand and won't let go. They're meaner than hell, and full of sharp teeth." The pike stiffened after the blow, then relaxed. "Now, all ya got to do is roll the pot licker in the sand awhile to get rid of the slime."

Tom, wanting to be a good student, naively picked up the fish by the gills. "Right here, Mr. Powers?" he asked, pointing to the ground.

Ike Powers and Anna laughed. "Nah, son, I was just kidding." Anna brought Powers a slender fillet knife from the cabin. Ike slashed it a few times against his leather belt to hone its edge. "Watch how I do this."

Powers slid the narrow blade into the firm flesh near the backbone behind the fish's head. Following the backbone, he directed it in a straight line until it met the dorsal fin, carving the fillet away from the rib cage on both sides. "See this line near the top? This is how you remove those nasty Y bones."

Powers did the first fillet while Tom watched closely. "Now, your turn," he said.

Tom did his best, but his fillet was a bit minced compared to Ike's. "Not too bad, Tom, you'll get the knack of it," Ike said.

Powers had a load of knowledge of how to be a good outdoorsman, how to be a survivor in the wild, he had done it in France and Germany as an elite soldier during the Great War. He knew how to be a killer, if he had to be, just as he had been in Europe not so many years before.

Tom took to him immediately, eagerly wanting to learn what the older man was willing to teach. They became the teacher and the student from that moment on.

Every day for the next week, the Vermonts and Ike Powers came to the club while the Harringtons went about enjoying mornings fishing and afternoons hiking through the oak and pine forest near the club. Anna made meals for them and tidied up, making beds and sweeping the floor. Even John seemed to be at ease reading aloud or else quoting from the teachings of Buddha: "I will teach you the Truth and the Path leading to the Truth" was one of his favorites.

Ike Powers and Tom spent much time together. With Tom he portaged a canoe down to Lake Frances where they caught trophy northern pike on nearly every cast. Powers showed Tom how to hone a knife, making it as sharp as a surgeon's scalpel. Tom held the oiled whetstone in his palm, its smoothness feeling like a baby's skin. He gently lashed the edge of the blade in delicate swirls until its sharpness could shave the fine hairs on his forearm. He taught Tom how to shoot the Model 12 pump shotgun by tossing empty cans in the air, coaching him how to lead the barrel ahead of the can so he could hit it in flight. There were a few duds in the old box of shells caused by the damp. Ike laughed when Tom flinched as he squeezed the trigger, anticipating the ensuing jolt that never came when the shell misfired. "Keep the stock tight against your shoulder and grit your teeth when you shoot. You won't feel the recoil as much," Ike said.

By the fourth day, the pleasant doldrums of a sunny afternoon set in, and Doctor Harrington sat in wicker chair inside the screened porch facing Shoepac Lake. He sipped on a glass of burgundy wine and drew deep puffs from a cigar. Such was his habit for relaxing. The family would have to leave the cabin and return home the following day.

Just beyond the cabin, where young oak trees had grown to ideal firewood size, Ike Powers was showing Tom how to fell a tree using a cross-cut saw. Tom found these lessons enjoyable and valuable in the event he was to come to the cabin by himself one day. Once the wood was sawn, split and put up in a neat stack near the cabin, the two rested. Both drank chilled well water from dented pannikins at the well head.

"There's a place I'd like to show you, Tom. It's a bit of a hike, and we probably won't get back here until sunset, but I know you'll like it. What do ya' think?" Powers asked.

Tom rose, ready to go at that moment. "Sure, anytime you're ready, Ike. Anything we need to bring?"

"Good question. You should always think ahead when planning a hike like this. Now, let's say we head out and, for some reason, we can't make it back before dark. What would we need to spend a night in the forest?"

Tom thought for a moment. "Well, we'd need to light a fire, I suppose. Maybe extra clothes if it got cold? Other than that, I don't know, Ike," Tom said.

"Good answer, but don't forget water. Always make sure you have water nearby. Having a hatchet and a knife are good tools to bring, too. Ask your father if you can go, and check with John, maybe he'll want to join us."

Powers walked to the pickup and fetched a hatchet and a short spool of rope in anticipation for the trip. He opened the door of the cab to get an oil-soaked pouch behind the seat, then pushed it inside his back pocket.

Tom returned to Ike Powers to report his father had given him permission to go. John, not surprisingly, had passed on the invitation.

Powers led the way to the shore of Shoepac Lake. They got in the canoe with both paddling toward its east shore.

Along that side of the lake rose a towering bluff, sheared sharply from the sand bank in a way that created a great wall nearly a hundred feet high. A colony of bank swallows darted and fluttered in and out of their tunneled nests all along its face, behaving more like bees than birds. Tom asked, "Have you ever been over there?"

"Yes, but I don't like to go there because it was used for centuries by the local Indians. It's kind of sacred to them. You shouldn't go there, either, Tom, out of respect, okay?"

"Okay, Ike. I won't," Tom said, paddling while at the same time he tried to observe the cliff for as long as their tack allowed. At the crest of the high cliff, a lone red pine stood perilously close to the edge, its roots emerging like a defiant skeleton clinging to the fragile sand.

When they reached the far shore, they dragged the canoe past the reeds and muck to store it safely on secure sand. There, they hiked farther to the east over sandy knolls and thick forests of pine and hardwood where there was no trail. Beneath a bright sun, they walked through thick patches of blueberry and wintergreen shrubs, stopping occasionally to look for berries, but it was too early for them to sprout. Two hours later, they reached their destination at the rim of an immense karst a mile wide and hundreds of feet deep.

Tom and Ike stood near its edge, and sopped the sweat from their faces with their sleeves. Below, popple treetops swayed, their leaves trembling with what wind reached them. Farther down the steep slope of the sinkhole, which had formed ten thousand years earlier, the trees stood still, the breeze failing to reach them.

"Incredible," Tom said through a soft breath.

"I knew you'd be impressed, Tom," said Ike Powers.

"What's down there, Ike?" Tom asked.

"Not many know for sure. Some say Shoepac Lake and this sinkhole were once used as an Indian burial ground. Good Indians were buried here. Maybe they believed their spirit was closer to the afterworld deep in the sinkhole. Bad Indians were dumped in the lake, never to return and do harm again. But getting to the bottom of this place isn't too difficult; it's the getting back that's a killer."

The two sat with their legs hanging over the edge with their heels making small amphitheaters in the sand that crumbled below their boots, both anticipating a trip down the jagged trail where erosion brought gnarly tree roots to the surface, like skeletons in some forgotten graveyard.

"We didn't come all this way to just look, did we, Ike?"

"Let's give it a go," Powers said.

Leaving their hiking necessities on the ground, they leaped into the sinkhole. Ike led the way. Their steps lengthened to broad leaps and bounds on the severe vertical slope of the washed-out trail. Soon they found themselves running wildly to keep upright. Tom stumbled half way down and began tumbling head over heels, unable to stop until Ike braced himself on a tree root and grabbed Tom by the waist. Then they slid and somersaulted farther into the sinkhole, their breath pounded from their lungs, until finally coming to rest in an awkward heap at its bottom. When they came to, Ike's right hand was twisted sideways, broken at the wrist.

"Damn!" he groaned, cradling his limp right hand across his lap.

Tom stood and began spitting out the mouthful of sand acquired during the fall. "Geezas Ike, look at your hand. You okay?"

Ike rose to his feet, inspecting the rest of himself. "Never mind me, are you hurt?" he asked Tom.

Tom checked closer. "I think I'm okay, just a mouthful of sand and a couple scrapes. I'm a bit dizzy, too. Geezas criminy, we have to get you out of here, Ike. My father can fix that wrist, I'm sure," Tom said.

Despite Ike's broken wrist, he urged Tom to explore the belly of the karst. There were no trails made by man or animal, only the remnants of a life cycle of pines and poplars that had grown and died off over the centuries. Left behind were the husks of their limbs and trunks to rot in the stifling heat rising from the sandy floor that fed life to new generations of their kind. Tom went farther inside the sinkhole, stepping over the bodies of dead trees, his feet sinking into the soft furrows of sand made by streams of rainfall that had shaped the ground in small, wavy deltas. He came upon an array of stacked limestone cairns, each carefully constructed with a wide base that narrowed to its crest that was waist high. He knelt beside them, touching the sun-warmed shards with his palms and fingertips, as though he were searching for a pulse, hoping they would speak to him, wondering who had constructed them, and when they were placed there. Tom whispered, "In the name of the Father, the Son, and the Holy Ghost," while he made the sign of the cross. He set out to return to Ike.

High above, where the moving sun had made the west side of the karst dark in shade, a raft of canvasback ducks whirled overhead, the wind beneath their wings singing acapella in the sky. Ike was where Tom had left him, sitting nestled in a sandbank, attempting to construct a cigarette with one hand. He toiled with the pouch of tobacco and its thin paper partner. Tom took over the project, handing him the wedged paper with the tobacco laid inside. Ike licked the edge and rolled it together with his good hand, like a professional.

"You found them, didn't you?" Ike said, the crinkled tube hanging comfortable from the edge of his mouth.

Tom sat beside Ike, his face dripping with sweat. "Yes, I found them, Ike. I felt like I was going back in time." Tom squeegeed the sluice of sweat from his forehead with the edges of his palms, "I was afraid if I stayed longer, they would speak to me."

"I think they did speak to you, son." Ike lifted himself from his hollowed seat in the sand. "It's time to go."

Climbing back to the precipice took hours. Ike, hobbled by the injury to his wrist that prevented him from hauling himself up the incline by the exposed roots and trees, removed his undershirt so that Tom could make a sling from it. It was a laborious and grueling climb out of the sinkhole, but they reached the upper edge while some sunlight remained.

"Whose idea was this?" Tom said through heavy gasps. They both laughed. They were exhausted. The sky was darkening with deep clouds that soon began to release a cooling rain.

"We're going to make camp, Tom. We could get lost trying to get out of here in the dark. Take the hatchet and cut some of those smaller popple trees to build a lean-to for shelter."

Ike retrieved the pouch from his back pocket that held a loaded Luger 9mm pistol he had brought back from the war, and set it on top of the pouch between them. Tom noticed it, and asked Ike how to use it. Ike showed him where the safety was, should he need to fire it. "Aside from that, just point and shoot," he added.

Tom cut four sturdy poles, trimming the branches away from their stocks. With Ike's guidance, he tied the poles tightly together with the rope Ike had brought. Ike collected deadfall branches to make a fire. Tom found a spruce tree and cut its boughs to layer over the lean-to. An hour later, they sat quietly near the fire, eating crumbling biscuits from the small bindle Ike had brought along, sipping water sparingly from Ike's dented canteen, digesting the day's events, while rain began falling more heavily.

"Try to get some sleep, Tom. At first light, we can head out. You'll probably have to do all the paddling," Ike said, holding his swollen wrist close to his chest. "I'm sorry about that."

"I'll get us back, Ike. Let me know if there's anything I can do for you," Tom said, curling up near the fire's edge, just inside the cover of the lean-to.

The evening wore on with the steady rain falling on the camp, but it remained dry inside the structure. They talked about the day's events as the last glimpse of light fell off to complete darkness in the forest.

Tom fell soundly asleep. Ike, still in elevated pain, dozed only intermittently. He became fully awake when the sound of a low growl came from beyond the campfire light. A pair of glowing eyes darted within the shadows, keeping its self from full view. Ike got to his feet and fetched a burning branch from the fire. His pistol was out of sight because Tom hadn't returned it to the leather pouch. Without the use of his pistol, Ike waved the burning branch back and forth as though it were a flashlight, a weapon. The coyote hunched and sprung into view, its teeth gnashing through a white froth drooling from its mouth. Ike screamed at the animal, but the coyote carried its attack straight on before Ike could find the pistol. Ike raised his good arm in defense and turned his back toward the crazed animal. The coyote sunk its teeth into Ike's back, viscously tearing at his flesh. With only the use of one arm Ike, did what he could to repel the animal. Tom awoke and rushed to the fray and pushed the pistol's barrel against the ribcage of the coyote and squeezed the trigger twice. The coyote yelped loudly and fell lifeless to the ground.

Ike lay on his back, staring into the falling rain. He'd been issued a death sentence, and he knew it.

"Get up, Ike, get up!" Tom pleaded. Ike rolled to one side and sat upright. The rain had soaked through their clothing; still, they remained sitting apart from the lean-to.

Ike said, "I'm a dead man, Tom."

"No, don't say that. You're okay, you're not dead. Come on, let's get back to the fire where it's dry." Tom lifted Ike to his feet, helping him back to the lean-to.

Ike's shirt was torn nearly from his back. He lowered his head, thinking what he should do next. Tom watched Ike, realizing he was in agony, but he felt powerless. The spring's night air was cold, their heavy breathing puffed in gray clouds before their faces, but both men were sweating from the exertion.

"I've only got one slim chance here, Tom. You're gonna have to help me, though. God dammit!" he shouted.

"What do you mean, one chance, Ike?" Tom asked.

"Did you see that animal's mouth, its teeth?"

"No, what about it? What about its teeth? I didn't see anything," Tom said.

"He's got the hydrophobe, Tom. Rabies! God dammit! That means I got it, too. There ain't no cure for rabies once it sets in, no cure a toll, son."

"Geezas, Ike, don't say that. My father can fix you, he's a great doctor. You'll see!" Tears formed in Tom's eyes. He began to pray to himself.

"There's one thing we can try, Tom. Get my knife and stoke up the fire until it's blazing as hot as the hubs of hell. You'll have to do this, Tom. You need to cauterize the bite area, all of the places where I'm bit. Do you understand, Tom? I need to count on you. That might kill the disease."

Tom lurched from Ike's side, scootching his rump in the damp sand, horrified with the idea of burning Ike. How could he bring himself to inflict such brutal pain on his friend? Tom's voice stammered, "I don't know if I can do this to you, Ike. There must be some other way?"

Ike's voice raised with contention. "It has to be done! This may be my only chance, Tom. Get that fire going, maybe I can do it myself. Just tell me if the knife is in the right spot."

Tom rolled his fingers together like a dying spider, making confident fists. "Okay! I'll do it!"

Tom built the fire where there was a raging bed of coals and flames. Ike had him place the blade of his knife on the coals until it was white hot. "Now lay the blade on the bite areas of my back, all of them.

Don't be afraid, Tom. We'll get through this," Ike insisted.

When Tom folded Ike's shirt away from his skin, the man's back showed the mangled scars from his injuries in the Great War. Ike had been severely burned during a battle, leaving most of his back in a contorted and grotesque scar. Tom held the blade ready. Ike screamed, "Do it!" Ike repeatedly cried out in agony each time the knife pressed against his skin. Wafts of smoke sprung from the blade, sizzling the flesh like bacon in a frying pan. The putrid, nauseating stench of Ike's seared skin filled the lean-to and made Tom vomit. Ike passed out from the pain, falling to his side near the fire.

When morning came, small flicker birds darted in an out of the lean-to searching for insects, their wings flitting, humming nervously, waking Ike and Tom. Ike admitted surprise at still being alive when he rolled on his side and rose from the sand. Tom sat upright and massaged the sleep remnants from the corners of his eyes with his knuckles. Tom smiled when he saw Ike standing, stretching the stiffness from his body, seemingly unfettered from their ordeal.

They struggled to make it back to the lake. Tom managed to get them across it paddling by himself while Ike did his best to steer from the rear of the canoe with his good hand holding an oar.

When they entered the cabin, something dreadful had happened while they were gone. Ned Vermont was sitting near the wood stove cradling an infant girl, tears running in a steady stream from his eyes. Anna lay lifeless on a bunk. A pool of blood seeped around her mid-section.

While Ike and Tom were gone, Anna had gone into a vicious labor. Doctor Harrington did what he could, but Anna just wasn't strong enough to withstand natural childbirth, and died before the baby was born. Doctor Harrington, with John as his assistant, was able to rescue the newborn by opening Anna with a scalpel. If he hadn't been there, the infant would have died.

Doctor Harrington began making coffee in a large percolating pot on the cook-stove. Tom and Ike told them what had happened on their trip. Tom held a bright lantern while the doctor inspected Ike's wound. The doctor gasped at the condition of the scars on Ike's back. "I've seen this before. I'm amazed you lived through it, Mr. Powers. What happened?"

"German flame-thrower," Ike said. "The day after the Armistice, 1918. My platoon was behind enemy lines in France when it happened. None of us knew the war was over yet."

Doctor Harrington inspected the crude cauterized area where the coyote had bitten the man. "Mr. Powers, I don't think its teeth broke through the heavy scar tissue. I'll be damned!" As a precaution, Harrington advised Powers to see a Rogers City doctor for immediate rabies treatment.

Anna was taken to Karr's Funeral Home, where she would be prepared for burial at Elmwood Cemetery. Anna's younger sister, Laura, had lost her husband two winters earlier when he was pulling a load of pine logs with a team of horses across Black Lake, and went through the ice. She would care for the child until Ned could figure out how he would manage raising her.

The Harringtons set out for the long trip back to Birmingham near noon on Sunday. It was a heavy-hearted goodbye for them.

The Motel T struggled over the brutal trail on its way to Rogers City. When they changed vehicles, they drove down Third Street on their way out of town. St. Ignatius Catholic Church was holding a late Sunday mass with a christening that followed. Its narthex swarmed with the departing congregation. The crowd separated for the newborn and his parents to parade through them, like royalty. John peered at them from his backseat window, reflecting on the death of Anna, and the birth of her child. He whispered the words of Buddha to the window, "Everything with a beginning has an ending."

.

Chapter Four

Times were bleak, people were poor and getting poorer around Detroit that May of 1930. Before the stock market collapsed and the economy crashed seven months later and ushered in the Great Depression, Delmar Spellman had been riding high with the good times, getting choice, well-paying assignments that brought him notoriety within the social circles of Detroit. He was well in demand until a lapse of good judgement had crippled his reputation. He was caught in bed with the wife of John R. Brown, a prized client, thus ending much of his ties with the Grosse Pointe upper crust. Spellman considered himself lucky, however; he had "serviced" many other affluent wives around town without public notice. Some of his competitors attributed his success to his keen, photographic eye; others said it was the considerable size of his manhood that brought him such favorable assignments. He was dark-haired, blue-eyed, handsomely thin, yet wide at the shoulders, and had the perfect teeth of a movie star. He was a successful negotiator of his services when dealing with the wives of his clients, using his flirtatious personality and handsome appearance like a company brochure.

    Delmar Spellman's photography studio was on the mezzanine above the Hotel La Salle's lobby, on Woodward Avenue in Detroit's cultural part of town. He was the hotel's photographer. Whenever hotel clients needed photographic coverage of an event, Spellman got the referral from the hotel's sales staff. The studio walls displayed his finest portrait photos in ornate frames of silver and gold gilding. The largest prints presented the city's most prominent citizens– Henry Ford and Ty Cobb, and Detroit mayor, Frank Murphy, each of whom sat before his lens. Behind his desk, however, there were glossy, mounted trophy pike and smallmouth bass he had pulled from Shoepac Lake over his years of membership at the club, which was something he was equally proud of.

A week earlier, Frank and Isadore Feinstein had come to his studio to hire him for a surprise birthday party they were giving their older brother, Ira. He knew of the Feinsteins reputation of being in an underworld mob, but the hotel was known to cater to men of such character around Detroit. The Feinsteins would pay him well for the two-hour assignment.

Frank Feinstein was particularly interested in the mounted fish, wanting to know where he'd caught them. Spellman boasted of the remote fishing club in northern Michigan, telling Feinstein the club was near the Straits of Mackinac and Lake Huron. Feinstein became even more interested upon learning this. They talked at great length about the club, and what it would take to become a member. Frank Feinstein said he would "reward" Spellman should the board look favorably on his family's application. Spellman said he'd be happy to help; he'd confer with the other board members about joining, being there was a need for new members. He didn't mention that the club had strict rules regarding the background requirement of being Protestant.

****

Hard times can lead men to rationalize their decisions by bending bylaws, thus corrupting the purity and intent of rules. Spellman brought up Feinstein's request at a board meeting a week later. Had the club's bank account been in better, shape there would likely have been resounding resistance, but such was not the case. Reluctantly, after long debate, they agreed to allow Frank Feinstein to become a member but not the other brothers. They wanted to see how one Jew in the club was going to work out. They granted Frank Feinstein a six-month trial membership.

"Jews in the club?" one board member of prominent Protestant doctrine remarked at the close of the meeting at the DAC. "What's next, wops and darkies? We're going to regret this. Geezas!"

*****

Under the dim orange glow of his safelights, Spellman tied the strings of his rubber apron tightly around his high waist, preventing photochemicals from getting on his suit. A half dozen trays holding developing chemicals sat on a long table near an enlarger where he was making "rush" photographs to be picked up in two hours by a different hotel client. When he was finished, he snugged his tie in a mirror and gave himself a once-over before going upstairs to the Feinsteins' evening photo assignment.

Spellman arrived on time to the seven o'clock party in the grand ballroom of the La Salle. He lugged his black camera bag that was bulging with two Speed Graphic cameras, a dozen four-by-five film backs loaded with black-and-white film, and a Graflex flash. The guests began arriving in clusters; nearly a hundred had been invited, all close associates of the Feinsteins, and most of them Jewish.

What Spellman thought would be a catalogue of simple table shots and grip-and-grin photo, as he called them, became a demeaning assignment for a photographer of his stature and skill. The arrogant Feinsteins treated him as a simple laborer, slipping five-dollar bills in his hand and ordering him to take photos of insignificant conversations and impromptu settings of intoxicated guests raising glasses in undignified poses with their yarmulkes pinned to their heads. But Spellman did what he was told and worked subserviently throughout the evening. He needed the money, so he could pay his studio rent, which was two months over due.

Irving Shapiro wandered unaccompanied from one conversation to another in the smoke-filled ballroom, carrying an ever-present cocktail of Scotch whiskey haphazardly in his hand, splashing it more frequently the drunker he got. On the stage, Jethro Copeland's big band played jazz loudly over the crowd. Guests danced joyfully across the ballroom floor, laughing with some changing partners midsong throughout the evening. Janet Olivet, a soft-complexioned, brightly dressed hotel cigarette girl, strolled about the crowd offering tobacco goods to the guest from the tray she held strapped over her shoulders. She was a lovely twenty-year-old downriver girl with sad but tempting eyes. The tray she carried did little to disguise her large breasts, which Shapiro became increasingly interested in. He followed her everywhere and wouldn't leave her alone. Janet tried to remain friendly, but as the evening wore on, Shapiro became more aggressive and began fondling her breasts. At one point, Spellman interceded by asking Shapiro to pose for a photo, allowing Janet Olivet an exit route, but Shapiro went after her again. Eventually, Olivet stood up to his crude advances and angered Shapiro enough to tear her dress at her shoulders, trying to expose her tits. Spellman tipped off Frank Feinstein, who told the girl to pack it in for the evening. He gave her a twenty-dollar tip for her troubles.

Spellman was requested to work beyond the two hours he was hired for, a request that felt more like a command from Frank Feinstein. Spellman had to go back to his studio for more film.

When the last guests departed, Frank Feinstein anticipated hearing good news about his membership acceptance to Shoepac Outing Club that evening.

All along, Feinstein thought Spellman was Jewish because of his last name. When Spellman told him he had good news, Feinstein was pleased, figuring, how else could he get them in to the club if he wasn't a loyal Jew?

But Spellman wasn't a Jew; he had taken his chances pretending to be Jewish by wearing a black yarmulke for the evening. He didn't admit the small detail when Frank Feinstein delivered two envelopes at the close of his assignment; one held his photo pay, the other contained two-hundred dollars for his membership referral.

The ballroom was now empty of guests. Spellman and the Feinsteins sat at a cleared table where Spellman spread out a detailed map showing how to get to the Shoepac Outing Club from Detroit, going over the topographic details carefully with Frank Feinstein. Frank wanted to get up north as soon as he could to enjoy the club, he said. But Feinstein had other plans for the club. Its remote location suggested a safer harbor to which he could run whiskey down from Canada; this promised a great expansion of the gang's operations.

The men left to take the elevator down to the lobby. Three floors down, a small crowd of hotel employees gathered around Janet Olivet, who was lying dead in a pool of her own blood, a result of her fall from high above. Her tray of tobacco goods was spread apart from her like pieces of a dropped dinner plate. Spellman paused, lowering his gear slowly near his feet; he couldn't take his eyes off Olivet, her lifeless body contorted and folded in an unnatural pose with her back broken and her left arm skewed at her elbow. The Feinsteins paused; only Frank and Shapiro recognized her as the cigarette girl who had been dismissed earlier. Shapiro bent for a pack of Chesterfields near his feet, and stuffed them in his suit pocket, as though he deserved them. He took Frank Feinstein's arm to usher him along, away from the gathering, away from the Detroit Police, who were coming through the hotel's main entrance. When Spellman's gaze met Shapiro's, he could see the murderous indifference seeping through the slits of his sleepy eyes, his poisonous character defiantly peering back at him without remorse. Spellman wanted to scream, "He did it!" but a fearful vision of him lying on the floor, like Olivet, prevented him from following through with it.

When Spellman returned to his studio he bolted the door behind him, pulling it several times to insure it was securely locked. He waited in the shadows behind the muted glass for a long time to be certain he hadn't been followed by Shapiro.

A month went by before the Feinsteins were able to engage their trip up north to Shoepac Lake.

Chapter Five

Early on the first day of June 1930, Doctor Harrington said goodbye to his wife, Helen, and got in his new Packard sedan to go to the hospital to check on a patient he'd operated on the day before. Dawn broke onto a cloudy Sunday morning. Harrington knew he needed to be back home in time for Tom's graduation from Baldwin High School that afternoon, and thought he had plenty of time. The previous evening, the Harringtons had hosted a soiree to celebrate their son's accomplishment. Queenie Harrington had provided the evening's entertainment by singing ragtime tunes and playing her new Steinway piano in the family's parlor. Doctor Harrington had gotten a special price on the expensive piano from Henry J. Linger, one of the Shoepac Club's board members. The family lived in a new, cream-colored brick Tudor Revival home off Quarton Road in what was still farm country within the city limits of Birmingham.

Doctor Harrington's drive to Beaumont Hospital took him down Woodward Avenue, a broad highway that led from Pontiac in the north all the way to downtown Detroit to the south. The hospital was two miles away in Royal Oak.

Helen Harrington, an athletic, good-looking woman in her mid forties, comfortably conjured the modest elegance she had developed as the wife of a prominent surgeon, and impressed folks via a young appearance that belied her age. Her easy going demeanor never revealed anger or fear; instead, she spoke softly and precisely in well-constructed sentences, with a grace that gave a calming effect on her children when necessary.

The family bustled about the home in preparation for Tom's graduation. Everyone was confident in what they would wear, except for Queenie, their sixteen-year-old daughter. Her revved up personality often tested Helen's patience and demure vernacular. Today would be one such occasion.

"Queenie, just wear the green dress. It's a graduation ceremony, not an audition. You will be gorgeous in whatever you choose, but especially in this one." Helen held the drab green buttress-shouldered dress against her daughter's defiantly framed stance. Queenie had preferred a suggestive purple flapper dress that clung tightly to her shapely body and ended just above her knees, along with a lengthy string of pearls her grandmother had given her on her sixteenth birthday.

"I'll look like you if I wear that one, Mother. Lordy! Fuck a duck, fer Chrissake!" Queenie bawled.

Helen kept her pose, and angled her head to one side. She replied, "I'm not going to fret about it, Queenie. Perhaps we can confer with Father when he gets home?"

Queenie crumpled the green dress and tossed it onto her bed, then pranced off in a huff, already knowing what her father would say. To underscore her protest, she took one of Helen's cigarettes from her smoking case, lit it, and waved it about, blowing a cloud of smoke at her mother while singing, "How ya gonna keep 'em down on the farm, after they've seen Paree'?"

"Good Lord!" Helen responded, coyly smiling after using her "Father" trump card.

After Tom's ceremony, the entire family celebrated by going for authentic Italian food at the Roma Cafe, on Riopelle in Detroit. Tom brought his friend Maxwell "Max" Milton, a tall, rangy boy with dark, coarse hair the shade and texture of knitting yarn that held no direction whenever he combed it without Brylcreem. When he smiled, his narrow face widened as though it had grown. Max was Tom's high school classmate and was also on the golf team, and he, too, was enrolled at Michigan State University for the fall, the same as Tom. They planned to room together.

They both shared a passion for the outdoors, yearning for its challenges, always ready for a chance to hunt and fish. Tom had told Max about the club, and Ike Powers and Anna Vermont, and what had happened to Powers at the sinkhole that spring. The story impressed Max, but also, he admitted, it filled him with jealousy and envy because he had yet to experience such events in his lifetime. He pressed his pleadings for Tom to take him up north the next time

Harringtons left for vacation at Shoepac Lake come the following day, Monday afternoon.

John Harrington sat at the round table twisting strings of spaghetti with his fork against a spoon. He paused with the fork near his mouth and said, "Father, there'll be room at the club for Max because I've decided I can't go this trip. He can have my bunk." The statement brought a gentle but excited bump of Queenie's shoeless foot against Max's crotch. She was smitten with Max, and quickly envisioned spending a week up north with him, though so far, Max had shown only disinterest.

Doctor Harrington expressed his disappointment in his older son and inquired why, suddenly, he was unable to accompany his family. "We've been planning this trip for a while, John. What are you going to do while we're gone? Your mother and I would like to have all of us up there at the same time."

"Yes, John, all of us. That includes you, dear," Helen said, setting her unlit cigarette in a vacant ashtray.

"I'm sure we would have a splendid time together, but there's a symposium Tuesday at the university, regarding Western existentialism compared to nihilism, as portrayed by the teachings of Friedrich Nietzsche, widely known as the father of this theory. I'm intensely enamored by his concept and want to better understand it. Did you know that some philosophies believe life to be devoid of objective meaning, without given purpose or intrinsic value? Imagine that. A stark contrast to Buddha's Brahmana reference that a mountain river takes everything with it, and never stops flowing, and that human life is like a mountain river. Fascinating, don't you think?"

Queenie rolled her eyes. "For heaven's sake. We surely wouldn't want you to miss *that*, John."

Doctor Harrington and the others tried to show attentiveness to John's interest, but the subject brought empty gapes to their faces.

Doctor Harrington said, "John, my first year at the University, I took an archeology course to fill out my semester class requirements. I found it fascinating, especially the field trips we went on. I was enthralled by exploring where ancient civilizations lived upon the very ground I was standing on while we searched out remnants of their past. I still find it intriguing, but I realized I could continue enjoying these places while following my true passion of becoming a physician. In other words, you can broaden your scope of thinking by studying the teachings of Buddha and Nietzsche without abandoning your true goal and passion that brought you to the university to begin with."

Tom reflected on his trip to the sinkhole, and the stone markers he'd found. "I experienced the same feeling when I saw the stone structures in the sinkhole, Father."

"Those markers are called cairns, Tom. Where I was raised in the UP, Indians have placed them all over the peninsula to honor the memory of their dead."

John dismissed his plate of spaghetti, nudging it toward the center of the table and then flipping his fork where it splashed against the red sauce and twine. "But, Father, what if this is my true calling? If so, surely you and Mother would want me to act on it?"

Helen, attempting to alleviate Johns frustration, commented, "Everything will work out for you, John. I believe in you, we all do, but I think your father's point is well taken."

Queenie leaned back in her chair, balancing a spoon on the tip of her nose. She let out a nasally, snoring sound while massaging Max's crotch again with her foot, enjoying the physical response she could tell she was eliciting from him–he certainly didn't appear to be so disinterested in her now. Her take on the topic brought laughter from everyone, save John and Max. John retrieved his plate. Max struggled to place the spaghetti fork to his mouth while enjoying Queenie's talented foot.

As often was the case, the Harringtons gave in to John's preferences and invited Max to join them up north, if he could get prepared in time. Doctor Harrington was adamant that they would leave at three o'clock the following afternoon. The trip would take twelve hours of steady driving, so they planned to spend the night at Doherty Hotel, in Clare, a Michigan town halfway to their destination.

Chapter Six

That Monday, Feinstein and Shapiro arrived at the small port town of Rogers City at noon with the top down on Frank's brand-new Cadillac Sixteen touring car. Seagulls screamed overhead, floating as effortlessly as kites on the warm breeze coming off the crystal-blue surface of Lake Huron. On the distant horizon, an ore freighter steamed downbound, leaving a billowy trail of black smoke. They had been driving for most of the night and were exhausted. They began searching for a place to get some sleep when they came upon the International Hotel, just off Third Street, downtown.

Frank parked the Cadillac near the hotel lobby entrance. They got out and stretched and went inside, wincing and blinking at the sudden change to dim lighting to find an apron-clad woman of middle age sliding a damp mop across the lobby floor. She smiled, noticing the Cadillac outside, their expensive suits. Feinstein and Shapiro looked starkly different from the usual sailors, loggers, and farmers she always saw around town. She asked, "Now, that's quite the jitney. We don't see many...cars like that up here, fellas. What can I help yous with?"

Frank explained how they'd been driving most of the night, and now were looking for something to eat and a couple of beds. "You got that here?"

"You betcha!" the woman replied.

It took a few moments for his eyes to adjust accordingly to the lobby's lesser light. He examined the room closely, as was his practice when entering any new place as he tried to account for possible threats and escape routes once he could see the room more clearly. Anchored to its tall, pressed-tin ceiling hung a pair of tired fans spinning slowly, churning the odor of fish throughout the lobby. There were paintings and photographs of wooden sailing ships, and steel freighters plowing through hazardous seas, hanging neatly on the wainscot walls. A full-size mount of a black bear stood in the corner near the stairwell that he assumed led to guest rooms on the second floor. An aged, wooden steering wheel was fastened to the wall behind the guest register counter. The woman brought the men to the counter, where Frank signed them in under false names. Feinstein said he was Mr. North; Shapiro was Mr. West.

The woman giggled. "Will Mr. South and Mr. East be joining yous soon?"

The men didn't flinch a hint of a smile. "Where is the dining room, ma'am?" Mr. North asked, his taut lips showing some irritation.

"Sorry, sir. It's right this way." She led them across the lobby and through a double set of doors to a narrow dining room in the back of the building.

The diner was the type of joint where rice was mixed inside the shakers to keep the salt dry and silverware was rolled tightly inside paper napkins. She seated them, brought menus, and poured them coffee from a steel pot; she seemed to be the only person who worked there.

"Today's special is baked whitefish, fresh caught by the Skipper, too, just like it is every day."

"Bring two orders… What's your name, ma'am?" Mr. North asked.

"Pricilla, but folks call me Miss Silly. I'll be back with your orders, shortly."

Miss Silly went to the kitchen. Mr. North and Mr. West tilted their heads and laughed. "Silly? What a name, oy vay!"

Inside the dining room were two patrons, a man and a woman of local appearance, the man wearing a work shirt with a name patch sewn over a pocket, and the woman was clad in a flimsy cotton dress suited for garden work. The tips of her fingernails were black with soil. Both were sipping from opaque glasses while eating fish sandwiches. Their gaiety and robust laughter suggested they weren't drinking ice tea. Mr. West was sure the glasses were dark because they held a liquid of "hushed" acquisition. When Miss Silly returned with their whitefish platters, Mr. West nodded toward the couple across the room and said, "We'd like a couple glasses of what those two are having, Miss Silly."

Miss Silly winked. "Be right back, boys. On ice?" she asked.

"Sure," Mr. West replied.

Miss Silly returned with two dark glasses of "imported" Seagram's whiskey. When she leaned to place the drinks on the table, she noticed the black handle of Mr. North's pistol he had holstered inside the open flap of his suit coat. She paused. "Ah, now you fellas wouldn't be government guys, would yous?"

Mr. West twitched his head toward Miss Silly. "Now, why would you think that, Miss Silly?" Then he noticed her staring at Mr. North's coat and the exposed pistol. "Aw, don't mind that. It's for personal protection. Hell no, we ain't G-men…Far from it, sister."

Miss Silly, feeling assured, set the glasses down and returned to the kitchen.

Mr. North took a sip from the glass. "It's the real deal, Mr. West."

"Are you thinking what I'm thinking?" Mr. West answered.

"Let's find out who the local merchant is," Mr. North said.

Miss Silly came back to the table with their bill. Mr. North called her close to him, and spoke in a low voice. "We are a couple...businessmen from the big city, Miss Silly. We're looking to improve and expand our inventory. Is it possible you could introduce us to the proprietor of this fine place?" He produced a five-dollar bill and nudged it toward Miss Silly, who pinched the bill and put it in her apron pocket.

"I'll see what I can do...Mr. North," Miss Silly said, then scuttered away out the back door of the dining room.

"Could we be this lucky to find a source for booze, right off the bat?" Mr. West asked.

"Don't get too excited yet. Because they got it here doesn't mean they're the source. Lots of these one-horse towns are getting it by hook or by crook," Mr. North said then he laughed. "By crook, I like that."

The men swirled the amber liquid in their glasses, sniffing and sipping to gauge its validity, waiting for the response Miss Silly would bring. When she returned she asked the men, "Come with me."

They followed her through the back door, and outside where the sun was bright. They were still squinting when she brought them to a small shed that was leaking a sweet-smelling smoke from a stovepipe on the roof. A weathered man, looking to be in his forties, stepped from the smokehouse in a long rubber apron. The sleeves of his bloodstained shirt were rolled back past his elbows, revealing sun-punished forearms and the fading tattoos naming the exotic ports he had sailed to when he was in the Navy during the Great War. His face was of the same ruddy shade. He wore a plain brown cotton cap that was tattered from excess wear on the brim. In one hand, he held a long, narrow fillet knife. Instantly, Mr. North and Mr. West reached for their pistols as casually as if they were grabbing a handkerchief.

"Settle down fellas," Miss Silly intervened. "This is Skipper—you know, the guy yous wanted to meet?"

The men relaxed, and Mr. North dropped his hand to the side. Mr. West kept his on the handle of his pistol, ready just in case. "Of course," Mr. North said. "It's a habit, a natural reaction when I see a man holding a knife, you understand."

Skipper smiled. "Oh, I'm cleaning fish. Sorry if I put a straw up yer' arses," he said with a laugh. "I'd shake yer' hands, but I don't think you'd care for my grip," he said, showing them his bloody, fish-scaled hand.

"I see, of course, sorry for the confusion, Mr. Skipper," Mr. North replied, wanting to get this introduction started off properly.

"Just Skipper. I'm cleaning whites for smoking," Skipper said.

After introducing themselves as Mr. North and Mr. West, Skipper jumped directly to the point, "Miss

Silly tells me yer businessmen from the city. What is it that interests yous?"

Miss Silly remained standing nearby. Mr. North removed his fedora, and looked her way. "Well, Skipper, we'd like to talk to you in private, if you know what I mean?"

Skipper gave a quick look to Miss Silly to dismiss her, and she bowed away back to the dining room.

"We've had a chance to sample your…your special drink in the dining room, and we're curious to know if you'd be interested in a business deal?" Mr. North said.

Skipper slid his fillet knife behind his belt, and walked over to a rain barrel near the smokehouse to wash his hands. He told the men he was an adventurous businessman in his own way, owning the International Hotel, and operating a successful commercial fishing business. But the men admitted it was his importing venture that interested them most.

"Go on, I'm listening."

Skipper took the men to his office where they could discuss a joint importing operation, one that would pay Skipper lots of money. They discussed the possibilities for over an hour. Skipper only revealed vague details of how he got his product to Rogers City. By the end of the hour, Mr. North and Mr. West revealed to Skipper their true names. Rather than shocking or scaring him, their information was needed to set Skipper more at ease; he said he had connections with an Anishinaabe Indian chief on the other side of the Straits who was his contact, but he gave no name. "I'll take you to meet the *Madame* here, shortly. She's a special lady, and has never let me down."

Skipper drove his pickup truck to the edge of town. The men followed him in the Cadillac to a calm cove near Seagull Point where Skipper introduced them to, the *Madame*, his fifty-foot fish tug vessel that was moored to a heavy beamed dock, with thick ropes fastened fore and aft keeping her still against the dock bumpers.

The *Madame* was as ugly as a boil. The boat's aluminum hull rose above its short midway deck, forming a rounded roof from her forward end to its aft end. At her aft end was a doorway where a thousand-foot net was coiled on a powered winch. The net was set out daily in the deep channel of the Straits of Mackinac where the whitefish congregated. An exhaust stack rose from the starboard deck, like a cylindrical spike had been driven through her by great force. The dull-gray diesel-powered fish tug was a Platz and Wenzel designed fishing vessel, constructed in Rogers City ten years earlier, and there was no better watercraft built to withstand the storms of the Great Lakes.

"She's brought me home many a time in the damnedest of seas, waves crashing on her like God's fists, winds over sixty miles an hour. And, she can hold lots of cargo!" Skipper bragged, as though the boat were a goddess, loved only by those who knew of such protections in a calamitous sea.

The men shook hands after their agreement. Skipper gave them a bottle of Seagram's as a gift. His first order was for as many cases of Canadian whiskey as the *Madame* could carry. Frank Feinstein would send for a truck to cart the whiskey back to Detroit.

Feinstein and Shapiro returned to the International Hotel to get some sleep. In the morning, they would make an unarranged visit to the club at Shoepac Lake. Neither of them had ever gone fishing before, or even set their feet on a boat.

When they went to the parking lot Tuesday morning to switch cars, the Ford Model T club car was not there. The men stood beside the Cadillac, pondering whether they should chance driving Frank's new car across the county. A moment later, a nosey local sheriff's deputy, having seen the rare automobile and the fancy suits marking them as out of place, stopped his police car. Feinstein and Shapiro stiffened, anticipating a possible confrontation. Cops approaching always meant trouble. They buttoned their suit coats to conceal their pistols. The bottle of Seagram's Skipper had given them was lying in plain view on the backseat of the Cadillac. Shapiro, showing more angst than Feinstein, turned his back to the officer, and quickly placed his fedora over the bottle. Feinstein, as usual, would do the talking.

Deputy McLennon stepped from his car. "Good morning, gentlemen. Is there something I can help yous with?" McLennon stared at the car, never having seen a Cadillac Sixteen. "Boy, that's some car, there. Sixteen cylinders! I bet she flies down the road, not like this old jalopy I'm driving."

"Why thank you, Deputy. I've only heard that she can run like the wind, but being a law-abiding citizen, I wouldn't think of it," Feinstein said.

Deputy McLennon winked, "I bet."

"Everything's fine here, Deputy…"

"McLennon, see?" pointing to his name tag above his shirt pocket.

"McLennon. Thank you. We're new members of the Shoepac Club, over by Onaway. There's supposed to be a club car here we can use to get there in, so we don't mess up the Cadillac," Feinstein replied, keeping his tone calm and friendly.

"Oh, hell, I know which car that is. It's usually here, but I bet she's over at A P Service getting worked on. That ol' girl gets a real workout. Tony, the owner, he's my cousin, you know." McLennon spoke as if the men should know the local blood-lines.

"You don't say?" Feinstein said. "Any chance we can find out for sure?"

"Why, that won't take but a minute. Jump in boys, I'll drive yous over to his shop, it's right down Third Street."

Feinstein and Shapiro looked at the police car with hesitation. For them to ride in a cop car meant spending time in jail. "Ah, maybe we better stay here, just in case it shows up while we're gone."

"Good thinking. How about I go over to the shop and check?" McLennon offered.

"Yeah, could you do that?" Feinstein replied.

The officer drove off promising to return with information on the club car. He returned in short time to tell them the car wouldn't be ready for a couple more hours, and they could wait for it over at the shop.

Feinstein and Shapiro decided they'd chance driving the Cadillac instead of waiting; there had been too much cop attention already.

Chapter Seven

The Harringtons had breakfast in the Doherty Hotel's restaurant early Tuesday morning. Aside from the fuss Queenie caused by ordering chicken embryos over easy, completely confusing the slow waitress, they got on the road unimpeded for the final six-hour drive.

They arrived in Rogers City and found the Ford Model T parked waiting where they expected it. A P Service had fixed a broken exhaust pipe and plugged a leaky tire, but it was nearly empty of gas. While Doctor Harrington filled its tank, Helen took photos of Tom, Queenie, and Max hanging on a giant ship's anchor displayed on the lawn of the courthouse. They drove off for Shoepac Lake in the middle of the afternoon.

It had rained through most of May, leaving the road to the club muddy with water covering it where it traced through the low lands. The Model T chugged and spun over the trail while making the difficult passage. It was very slow going, though the trail showed evidence of a car having traveled over it recently. There were deep ruts left behind, and scrapes in the center of the road where the preceding car had bottomed out in the deep, water-filled potholes. The Model T toiled in the same manner, weighted down with its luggage and passengers.

When the Harringtons reached the cabin, Feinstein's Cadillac Sixteen sat nearby in a mess. It had taken on the color of the road, with sandy mud packed in its wheel wells, its right front fender dented. Tom saw the long, horizontal scrapes along the length of its sides where tree branches had brushed against it, mentioning, "Who would sacrifice such a fine car for a fishing trip?" Just then, Feinstein and Shapiro stepped from the cabin, each holding a tin cup containing their second fill of Seagram's whiskey.

Doctor Harrington got out of the Model T puzzled. He hadn't expected anyone other than Ned Vermont or Ike Powers at the cabin. Did he get the wrong information on his reservation, he wondered? "Gentlemen, we are the Harringtons. I hope I got my reservation correct. Are you occupying the cabin beyond today?"

Frank Feinstein and Irving Shapiro, having the fast encroaching boldness provided by the whiskey they were drinking, implied the Harringtons must have made a mistake. Shapiro replied, telling a lie. They had never asked the club's board to reserve the cabin, they'd just showed up. "It seems you got it wrong, Mr...what did you say your name was?"

"Harrington, and this is my wife, Helen." Harrington, showing confusion, searched his surroundings, quickly darting his eyes. "I don't know how that could happen. We've had this week booked since May."

"Well, I don't know what..." Shapiro said, shifting to an irritated stance.

The calmer Feinstein interrupted before Shapiro could lead them into a quarrel. The Feinstein crew got their way by means of force most every situation they were in. Frank Feinstein took a milder approach, thinking this was not the place to have a pissing contest. He was on a six-month probation, too. They didn't need there to be any trouble with their first visit to Shoepac Lake, and he knew how to mellow Shapiro's temper. Their newly formed alliance with Skipper was too important.

"I think we're getting off on the wrong foot, Doctor Harrington. I'm Frank Feinstein, and this is my business associate, Irving Shapiro." Shapiro glared "hello." "Pleased to meet you." Feinstein went on, "And there won't be a problem, Doctor. I'm a new member here. This is our first visit, and I must say it's everything Spellman said it would be." He looked over to his damaged Cadillac. "Even the road from Rogers City, did you see my car? I sure as hell won't drive it here again. I'm sure we can work something out, folks."

Doctor Harrington, concealing his skepticism, stepped forward to shake hands with the men, and introduce his family and Max, who had darted off for the dock on Shoepac Lake already. Shapiro watched Queenie closely and with interest as she lagged behind Tom and Max. "We'll make do, I suppose. How long do you intend to stay, Mr. Feinstein?"

Feinstein looked at his Cadillac again. "Well, I don't think very long. I believe I damaged something under the car on the way here. I better get it over to A P Service and have Tony take a look at it. Have you met Tony yet? He's a cousin to Deputy McLennon, a Presque Isle County…police officer," Feinstein said, using his newly acquired local knowledge.

"Deputy McLennon? No, I can't say I have," Harrington replied, repeating the deputy's name to himself, committing it to memory, should he need to recall it.

"How about a drink, Doctor? Maybe Helen would like one, too," Feinstein asked, furthering his attempt to ease the uncomfortable situation.

Feinstein and Shapiro helped carry their luggage to the cabin. Inside, Feinstein poured whiskey for them in small tin cups. Feinstein urged them to bring their cups together, where he said, "To the club, lehayim!"

Tom and Max returned from the lake, rushing into the cabin as though being chased by a devil. A short moment later, Queenie, drenched in lake water, followed closely behind brandishing a black water snake as though it were a weapon. "You evil twats! Pot lickers!" She shouted, the snake coiled around her wrist with its head pinched between her fingers. She sprinted to Max, who was holding his hands in front of his face in an attempt to protect himself from the snake. Queenie waved the snake at Max.

"Whoa, what's going on?" Doctor Harrington said, trying to conceal a laugh.

Queenie stood within a pool of water that was collecting around her shoes, still holding the snake. Her wet clothes clung tightly against her body, revealing her woman's-size breasts and the shapely contours of her figure, like a hand inside a tight glove. Irving Shapiro held his lustful eyes constantly on her body until Feinstein nudged him to stop staring. Queenie continued pinning Max against the wall with the snake. "We were on the dock, and I saw the snake in the lily pads. I bent over to pick it up, and these cunts pushed me in!" She shoved the snake closer to Max's face. "How do you like that, Mr. Shit Head?"

"Queenie, please take that reptile outside, and let it go…please? Watch your language, too!" Helen said, calmly crossing her arms while shifting her weight to one side. "For heaven's sake. And, take it to the woods. I don't want any surprises when I use the bathroom facility. Your suitcase is on that bunk, change into some dry clothes."

"I hope you two will sleep good tonight," Queenie said, miffing a sarcastic smile. "You never know what you might find in your beds." She really wasn't mad at Max; for Queenie, this was flirting.

"*Well*," Helen said.

"Well what, Mother?" she asked.

"Sleep well tonight, not sleep good."

"Oh, I think I made my point *good*, Mother." Queenie tossed her head back, and took the water snake outside to release it.

Helen brought Queenie dry clothes while she was outside. She changed into them in the privacy of the north side of the cabin, away from the others' view.

When they returned to the cabin, Shapiro was standing beneath the low overhang of the porch, tin cup in hand, on the lookout for a chance to steal a glimpse of Queenie while she changed clothes. Frank Feinstein, always aware of impending trouble, stepped from the cabin and joined Shapiro to keep him civil. The women passed by, entering the cabin, smiling, yet unaware of Shapiro's unscrupulous penchant for young girls.

Inside the cabin, the men continued to drink whiskey, and held conversation about what they did for work as the afternoon waned. Feinstein and Shapiro spoke in diluted terms of their business, telling the Harringtons they were purveyors of entertainment and owners of lesser-known restaurants within the city. They said they dabbled as importers of "special" products for their exclusive clients.

Queenie perked her attitude overhearing the men say they were in the entertainment business, her passion. She moseyed about the cabin while the men chatted about fishing, the Great War, and the fine cigars they puffed on. She waited for an appropriate time to ask one of the men questions about their business. Maybe she could get an audition, she contemplated, but she would have to ask without her parents hearing. They would not allow it if she were to get a chance to sing and play in some downtown establishment. She waited until the men drank more whiskey before she would make her move. She would create a memorable vocal performance when the time was right.

An ooga horn rattled its metallic honk outside the cabin. Ned Vermont and Ike Powers were stopping by in Ned's pickup to check on the Harringtons. They brought a black cast-iron kettle full of chicken-stew that Ned's sister-in-law, Laura, prepared, should they be hungry. The two men knocked on the screen door, and Helen let them in. "Good afternoon, folks," Ned Vermont said. Noticing Feinstein and Shapiro, he remarked, "I see you brought some guests with you this time, Doc."

Doctor Harrington introduced Helen, and then the new member, Feinstein, and Shapiro as his guest. "There was some confusion about the reservation this week, Ned. Mr. Feinstein had the place booked, too. But, it'll all work out. They're leaving soon. Right, Mr. Feinstein?"

Irving Shapiro bristled at Harrington's assumption, but Feinstein kept it calm. "That's right, Doc. We'll head back to Rogers City soon. This was just a quick trip to check out the digs ups here."

Vermont frowned. "That's odd. I had you booked this week, Doc. Yeah, there musta been another spoon in the soup at work downstate, ay? Oh, Laura made yous some chicken-stew, hope yous are hungry." He set the kettle of stew on the table.

"Thank you, Ned. Tell Laura we thank her, too. Say, would you two like a taste of the good stuff we're having? Compliments of Mr. Feinstein and Mr. Shapiro. Sorry, I can't name its origin," Harrington offered, and then laughed regarding the Seagram's bottle sitting in open view.

"I'm punched in on the clock, Doc. Another time," Vermont said.

"I never touch the stuff, Doc," Powers replied, suspiciously eying the men from Detroit, especially Shapiro, who seemed to be constantly watching Queenie, who had curled up on a bunk bed.

Feinstein raised his cup for another toast. "Too bad we don't have some entertainment for this special afternoon, it would be very fitting."

That was all Queenie needed to hear. This was her chance. She sprung from her bunk and brushed a quick hand to her clothes and hair, preparing herself for an impromptu performance. "Mr. Feinstein, I believe there's a song that fits the occasion." Queenie subtly cleared her throat and began singing the Leo Reisman and His Orchestra tune, "Happy Days Are Here Again."

Queenie made the best of her opportunity to perform, dancing along in an impromptu skit while singing perfectly, joyfully, and with great composure. Everyone in the cabin took a seat and watched her closely. Her joy in performing infected her audience.

When she finished, her audience stood and applauded. Queenie bowed gracefully, grasping her hands tightly together. She knew she had done well.

Feinstein and Shapiro, smiling broadly, were still clapping slowly in approval after the others had stopped. "Helen?" Feinstein remarked. "I believe you have a budding star here. She's a natural. I think she has a great future in show business. Believe me, I've seen a load of auditions before, and her performance was splendid."

Queenie blushed at all of the praise, and humbly thanked Feinstein and the others. When she stepped out of the cabin, she made two fists, silently mouthing, "Yes!" Helen had left her whiskey cup on the armrest of a porch chair, along with her pack of Camels. Queenie gulped the whiskey down, wincing brightly as the liquid burned its way to her stomach. She reached for the Camels and filched one, lighting it with the flame of a Dunhill lighter. She walked to the privacy of the cabin's north side to smoke it. It wasn't her first cigarette.

"Caught ya…" a voice said from behind her. Irving Shapiro.

"Oh, shit!" Queenie said, surprised, trampling the cigarette under her shoe.

"Don't fret about it. I was your age when I started." Shapiro reached in his suit pocket, "You want to try these?" He said, holding out a pack of Chesterfield cigarettes.

Queenie, her mind whizzing from the whiskey and the cigarette replied, "Sure. Maybe I can finish this one." Shapiro tapped one end of the Chesterfield against his lighter to pack the tobacco tight, handing it to Queenie. She laughed and cupped her hand over Shapiro's while he lit her cigarette. She released a timid cough after taking a puff.

"So, you think you'd like to be a professional singer? We think you'd be a shoo-in, Queenie," Shapiro said. He handed her a business card. "How would you like to sing with a band behind you? Give me a call when you want to talk about it. I can put you to work right away. I've brought a lot of young talent to the big leagues over the years. But first, we'll have to have some professional photographs taken of you. Your official mug shot. I know just the guy who'll take it, Delmar Spellman. Ever hear of him? He's famous around Detroit." He laughed, thinking about his ignoble mug shot that was on display in every Detroit Police precinct.

Queenie took his card and pocketed it quickly, like she was stealing it. She gushed, "If my parents knew I had the chance to sing on stage, they'd have a cow!" She took a deep draw from her cigarette, contemplating quickly how she might take advantage of the offer. She was now desperate to follow her dream. Shapiro had presented her a solid opportunity to get started. She reasoned she would do anything to make it happen. She flitted her eyes, and begged Shapiro, "Please don't tell them about this, Mr. Shapiro. I'll call you when I get back home."

Shapiro's mind was planning, too. He pursed a sly smile, taking her hands in his, squeezing them gently. Shapiro tensed, feeling her soft hands within his. He brushed the backsides of his hand against her breasts. Queenie didn't flinch, regardless of the intrusion; she would allow it for the sake of the opportunity she was given. "Don't worry, Queenie, the secret is safe, okay?"

Queenie and Shapiro parted, both returning separately to the cabin so as not to raise suspicions.

The late-afternoon sun striking the tall pine trees draped protracted shadows over the cabin when Feinstein and Shapiro got in the Cadillac to return to Rogers City. Doctor Harrington, Ned Vermont, and Ike Powers stood near the roadway and watched as they drove off.

"I'm sorry those guys showed up, Doc. I don't believe they had a reservation. There has never been anyone showing up here by mistake," Vermont said, watching the Cadillac diminish into the forest.

Ike Powers said, "I don't like 'em, Doc. There's something fishy about those two. Especially that high-talkin' guy, Shapiro."

Helen Harrington found what she needed in the cabin to set the table for Laura's chicken-stew dinner. She invited Vermont and Powers to join them, but Vermont said he had to get back and help tend to his daughter; they would return in the morning.

Chapter Eight

The *Madame's* bow plowed and pushed her way through the choppy Lake Huron water, plotting toward the calm channels of the Les Cheneaux Islands with Skipper at the helm. A small white flag hoisted atop the bow spar hung motionless until an occasional whisper of wind jiggered it to life. The white flag was a signal "all is well" when he arrived at his destination. The diesel engine chugged at quarter speed, running quietly, the midmorning sun showing the submerged boulders lying below the aluminum hull in the shallow water. He was familiar with the tricky passage between Little LaSalle and Marquette Islands, having coursed through them so many times, and knowing about the countless vessels that had gashed their hulls against the rocks, but he had local knowledge taught to him by his Indian partner, Chief Louie.

Schools of perch dashed away from the hull of the *Madame* as she weaved her passage through the thirty-six-island chain. Today's mission was not to catch fish but to meet with Chief Louie Boivin.

Fifty years old, Louie the Thief as he was known around St. Ignace and Mackinaw Island gained the name because of his history of tainted dealings around the docks, mostly dished out to naive visitors who came to the area from Chicago and Detroit on flashy yachts, whimsically searching for authentic Indian items, historical treasures, and unscrupulous, indigenous women. Louie the Thief was a mixed-breed Indian of Métis, Anishinaabe and French heritage. He was the height of a drooping clothesline. His skin was the color of tannin-stained water. His high cheekbones bulged beyond his sunken eye sockets like brown copper buttes sloping toward the corrugated skin folds near his eyes.

Louie was raised on a St. Ignace reservation and was industrious by nature, making considerable profit by his creative enterprises. He employed a bevy of Anishinaabe squaws to make bows and arrows, and blankets and crude carvings, then sold them as historical artifacts. He knew how to get whiskey from Windsor, Ontario, too, by means of the many Anishinaabe and Ojibwe Indian tribes. There were loads of Indian reservations dotting northern Michigan and the Province of Ontario, from Windsor all the way to Sault Ste. Marie, in the Upper Peninsula of Michigan.

Skipper steered the *Madame* slowly into a hidden cove between two small islands. Louie Boivin squatted cautiously near the ground but rose calmly from his campfire after seeing the white flag. Standing at a close distance behind him was a tall, serious Anishinaabe Indian, appearing to be of an age beyond a youth. At his side was a rusted single- barrel shotgun. He cupped his hand over its business end, suspiciously watching Skipper and the *Madame*. Two snowshoe rabbits hung strung together, dangling at his side. He knelt and began skinning and gutting them, so he could skewer their carcasses on a steel spike to roast above the fire. Louie Boivin spoke to the younger man, who was his son, Aandeg, meaning "crow" in Anishinaabemowin. "It's okay, stay here." Boivin walked out on the wooden dock made of cedar planks nailed on oak stringers that were lag-bolted to sunken cedar posts. The dock was rigid and strong, built to hold the weight of men carrying heavy loads. Skipper shut the engine down, then reached for the coiled bowline lying on the deck. The *Madame* limped toward the dock. Skipper tossed the line toward Boivin where he tied it to a dock piling.

"*Boozhoo*," Skipper said, greeting Louie the Thief in Anishinaabemowin, his native language. "Are the bees in the hive?"

"Yes, the bees are home," Louie replied, looping the bowline around a dock post. Behind Louis sat fifty cases of whiskey obscured by a thick fishnet covering them.

"Good to hear," Skipper said, stepping onto the dock. In one hand he held an envelope filled with cash; in his other hand, a pry bar. The cash would pay Louie for the fifty cases of whiskey his men would load on the *Madame*. The pry bar was used to raise the lid on a case or two to inspect the sealed bottles. Louie's reputation called for verification on his shipment. The first delivery had gone well, and Skipper and Louie had made a healthy profit.

Unlike the first shipment, this load would be delivered to Duncan Bay, outside of Cheboygan.

Duncan Bay was twenty nautical miles closer than Seagull Point, near Rogers City, thus limiting Skipper's exposure of being caught by the Coast Guard, or rough seas that could damage the *Madame* or the fragile cargo. Feinstein's men would be waiting with a cargo truck at Duncan Bay. It would be a swift handoff.

Louie raised his hand, motioning to the half dozen ragtag men who were waiting within the cover of thick cedar trees to begin bringing the cases to the boat. The men were dark- skinned like Louie–young Anishinaabe "Indian bucks," as Skipper called them. Aandeg remained at the fire to attend the roasting rabbits.

After Skipper inspected several cases of whiskey, the remaining cases were loaded on board the *Madame.* Louie was handed the money envelope. He pawed through the bills in a brief but accurate counting. All the money was there. Louie smiled and said, "*Megwich.*"

"Same thing next week, Skipper?" Louie asked.

"As far as I know. I haven't been told otherwise. Keep it coming, Louie."

Louie looked at the dark clouds gathering in the west, studying them for a moment. "Better not dally around, Skipper. There's gonna be a blow coming in soon."

The Runners

Skipper shoved the *Madame* away from the dock and stepped aboard, her engine idling quietly until she pulsed ahead once he shifted to "forward." Skipper smiled, repeating the Anishinaabe word, *megwich*, meaning "thank you."

By the time Skipper left the calm island chain, Lake Huron was beginning to swell and roll under the building western wind. The *Madame's* hull slammed against the heightening waves, a hammer against a spike. But this was nothing new to her; she was designed to be in its company.

Chapter Nine

Irving Shapiro leaned back in his leather chair inside his second-story office overlooking the loading dock of an east side warehouse. Trimming his fingernails, letting the clippings collect in his lap, they would fall to the floor once he stood again, leaving them for Eloise, a black cleaning woman the Feinsteins employed for what Shapiro called "peasant work." He waited for the cargo truck to arrive with the Canadian whiskey aboard. Frank Feinstein entered the room without knocking.

"Seen the truck yet?" he asked.

"It should be here any time now." Shapiro rose from his chair and brushed the clippings from his lap. His desk phone rang and he answered it on the second ring–Shapiro never answered before the phone rang twice. He considered himself too dignified to answer it on the first ring.

A diminutive voice spoke on the other end. "Mr. Shapiro? Is this you?"

"Yes, who is this?" he replied.

"Quine Harrington. You know, Queenie? I sang for you at the lake cabin two weeks ago. You gave me your business card." On the phone, her small voice made her seem even younger than the girl he remembered.

Shapiro held up one hand and cupped the phone with the other to speak with Feinstein. "I'll be right with you, Frank. I've got to take this call."

"Just let me know when the truck gets here," Feinstein said, closing the door behind him. Shapiro nodded.

"So, how's the little songbird doing? I'm delighted you called, Queenie. Are you ready for an audition? I'm serious, you let me know and I'll make it happen." Shapiro pictured the way her wet outfit had clung to her young body that day in the cabin; he felt excitement and more than a little surprise, as he'd never thought he would hear from her.

"That's why I'm calling. When would it be a good time to have the audition?" Queenie asked, and paused, and then added apologetically, "I'll still have that slight problem of not telling my parents, remember? They're leaving town tomorrow for Chicago. My father has a seminar to attend, and Mother's going with him. Can we do it while they're out of town?"

Shapiro's devious mind went to work quickly, thinking of a scheme of deception Queenie could use to meet with him. "Let me handle that," he said, "and don't you worry. Once you get here, and we get you rolling with your first performance, I'm sure your parents will be proud of you, seeing you on stage, folks clapping and cheering. I'm going to make you a star, Queenie. You know that singer you like so much, what's her name, Ruth Etting? She's got nothing on you, sister. You'll be even a bigger star than her. I can make that happen, you know. What do you think about that?"

Shapiro could hear Queenie's excited breathing carry through on his phone. He was just as excited, knowing he'd have a chance to corrupt her with alcohol and other temptations, just like he had done to so many naive girls susceptible to promises of stardom. He would be patient with Queenie.

"This is so wonderful, Mr. Shapiro. I can't tell you how grateful I am. How can I ever repay you for this incredible opportunity?"

"Don't worry about that right now, Queenie. Just keep singing and practicing so you'll be ready," he said, leaning in his chair so he could examine the long wall mirror looking back at him. "Hey, start thinking about how you're going to spend the money you'll make singing down here, too. After all, that's what comes with the job, you know."

"Money, too? Heck, I'd do it for nothing just to get the chance to live my dream. Thank you, Mr. Shapiro."

"Are you available this Friday, say five o'clock? I can pick you up and bring you here? I'll get you back home in a jiff, no one will know. How's that sound?"

Queenie didn't pause to think it over, answering yes immediately. She would make good of the opportunity. Shapiro would pick her up at a coffee shop on Woodward Avenue, a short distance from her home.

A canvas-covered freight truck drove through the vacant loading area and backed into the loading dock below Shapiro's office. "See you at five on Friday, Queenie."

He hung up the phone and proceeded to the dock to inspect the freight, stopping by Feinstein's office to let him know the whiskey had arrived.

Fifty cases of Seagram's were set in rows, side by side, not stacked. Two of Feinstein's men began prying the lids from the cases to examine the contents of each, one by one, leaving nothing to chance. They paid a premium for this whiskey and expected it to be pure and unadulterated. One of the men pulled a bottle from its packing and paused, frowning, before handing it over to the bosses. The seal was broken, it had been opened. Shapiro swore and lifted another bottle himself; its seal was split, too. "We've got a problem, Frank," he murmured.

Feinstein used the first bottle to point to the worker that had handed it to him. "Check those over there, too. Check 'em all." Already Shapiro had removed his suit coat and begun to open another wooden case with a claw hammer. When all the cases were inspected, they found half of the bottles had been opened, appearing pale compared to the pure whiskey.

Louie the Thief had done a number on them, thinking he could get away with cutting half of the whiskey with Lake Huron water, keeping the other half for himself. What Louie didn't know was whom he was swindling. A grave mistake on his part.

Chapter Ten

The small bell above the entry door to Delmar Spellman's studio jingled when it opened Thursday afternoon. Spellman glanced up at the door, and the usual brightness of his face dulled when Irving Shapiro walked in. Spellman was with a potentially new client, a woman of importance from Grosse Pointe where he still had a few clients. She was a busy, fidgety, and distracted socialite who seemed to place great importance on the appointment book she fussed over while trying to figure out what day would be best for the portrait sitting she was trying to book with Spellman. She repeatedly apologized for the small red wine stain appearing at the hem of her peach-colored afternoon dress that blossomed in white furls over her small shoulders, leading to her elegant, wavy blonde hair. Sarah Trace was wife to a much older husband, the well-known automobile parts manufacturer, Emerson Trace. "Take your time, Mrs. Trace. Please excuse me for a moment." Spellman paused his flattering attention to her, telling Shapiro he'd be with him momentarily.

Despite his constant need for work, he didn't like the prospect of doing another photo shoot for Shapiro or the Feinsteins. Shapiro's sullen face brought to mind the still face of Janet Oliver on the sidewalk outside of Frank Feinstein's birthday party; he felt sure Shapiro had helped her over the third-floor railing that night, though Spellman had no way to prove it. He despised and feared Shapiro, but he was in no position to consider turning down his business. The dire need for money would compromise his fragile business integrity. Screwing his clients' wives was not considered *business* so much as an amenity.

Spellman escorted Sarah Trace to the glass door leading to the hotel's mezzanine, making sure Shapiro wouldn't have an opportunity to engage her in conversation. The doorbell jingled again as she departed. He returned to find Shapiro studying a large portrait of a lovely woman displayed in a gilded frame that took up a sizable portion of the wall.

"Ruth Etting," Spellman said, "She sat for me when she was a 'nobody,' but I could see her potential. I'm lucky to have had the chance to take that."

"Same Ruth Etting I hear on the radio?"

"Indeed," Spellman replied.

Shapiro came directly to the point. "I need something like this for a new singer I'm bringing to the business. She's young, but lots of potential. You should hear her sing. She's got it, I tell you. Now, I want to bring her by tomorrow around six, you see. And, I need photo prints of her for display around town by Saturday. Not big ones like this, but the smaller ones, ten by twelves, or something like that, whatever the standard is. Do you think you can handle that?"

"Eight by tens, you mean. That's the normal publicity-size print." It annoyed Spellman to learn of Shapiro's ignorance about such matters. "I'll need to bring in a makeup artist and hair stylist, you know? I can't get this kind of photo without her having makeup on. She'll look lifeless when I put lights on her, flat-skinned, no facial definition."

"I don't care what it takes, just do it. You're the photographer. Don't bother me with the particulars. Understand?" Shapiro said, his response blunt and nearly indignant.

Spellman bristled inside but remained calm. He calmed himself further by mentally running down some of the very particulars he wouldn't bother Shapiro with—each one a different number. If he took the assignment he would charge extra for the short turnaround, extra for the makeup and hair-styling artists, and extra for having to deal with an asshole. Spellman knew his business and knew how to make a client feel like he was getting a deal. He quickly studied the situation before deciding what his fee would be.

"I would love to handle this for you, Mr. Shapiro, but I have to look at my schedule book first." Spellman went to his desk, where he opened a bound datebook containing his assignment bookings. He flipped the book open. The pages were empty. No assignments that week. He studied the empty pages, mumbling indecipherably before he spoke. He proceeded to concoct a scenario of certain conditions that Shapiro would have to agree to. "I see I have a slight problem with that time. Mrs. Brown is scheduled for a portrait at six o'clock. She's already put a deposit down. I can call her to reschedule, but she might insist on a refund."

Shapiro scoffed. "Call her, I don't give a damn. I need this girl's photo, pronto."

"I don't know if she'll rebook, she's going out of town, and I don't know when she's coming back. That's a hundred bucks I'll forfeit," Spellman said.

"I'll cover that. Now, how much will all this cost? Bottom line," Shapiro demanded.

Spellman mumbled numbers, taking into account the rush photo fee, the cancelation fee, the makeup artist and hair-stylist fees, and adding lastly the asshole fee. Smiling, he told Shapiro he was going to give him an unheard-of discount on his services because he was a previous customer in good standing, "Five hundred dollars, Mr. Shapiro." he added, "Prints are extra, of course."

Shapiro was no fool; he knew Spellman was fleecing him, but he still said, "Okay," without the slightest hesitation. It wasn't that he couldn't afford it; he was carrying a coiled roll of money in his pocket the size of a beer can. It was his vulnerability, his need, that Spellman had taken advantage of, something he had always done to others.

"That's good, sir. Now, what is my client's name, so I can write her in the assignment book?" Spellman asked.

Shapiro realized Spellman would likely know who Queenie Harrington was; the Harrington name was known at the Shoepac Lake Club, and beyond. He couldn't let that happen. "Her name is Little Dove. Yeah, just call her Little Dove."

Shapiro pulled the bulging roll of money from his pocket and peeled off five one-hundred-dollar bills and gave them to Spellman.

"Would you like a receipt?" Spellman asked.

Shapiro glared. "I was never here. Remember that. And remember to forget about Little Dove coming here, too! Do you understand?"

"Perfectly," Spellman said. He watched Shapiro walk quickly to the door without another word, disappearing into the mix of people meandering about on the mezzanine. Once the man was clearly out of earshot, he wondered aloud, "What am I getting in to with this asshole?"

Spellman began working at his desk, going through a pile of unpaid bills, setting aside the ones that needed immediate attention. The small doorbell jiggled again. Sarah Trace entered, her face reflecting a certain glow of promiscuity he was so familiar with. She spoke in an alluring tone. "Delmar…you know I've always wondered what went on in a darkroom. Can you show me?"

Spellman smiled. "Of course. I'm just getting ready to make some photos. Would you like to see how they're made?"

"I would love to." She smiled.

Spellman turned the deadbolt on his studio door and reversed the "open" sign on the window. He turned the lights off. The sudden rise of lustful passion came over him, extending within his trousers. Sarah noticed his excitement and reached to feel him. They embraced in the blushing fall of light from the mezzanine.

He led her to the cot he kept at the flank of his darkroom, a cot he used to catch a few hours of sleep during late nights at work, and for opportunities such as Sarah Trace's visit. Passing his darkroom, he mentioned, "This is where I make photos on an enlarger."

Sarah regarded his arousal again. "I can't help but notice your personal enlargement, Delmar. What size is it?"

Spellman took her hand to his pants zipper. "The ten-inch variety."

"Oh, I see." Her voice weakened, stroking her hand along the length of his swelling, "I've never seen a print of this size before."

Delmar Spelling used his "enlarger" two times before Sarah Trace, limp in the legs and exhausted, departed as one of his happier clients. She assured him she would return again should he want to continue his darkroom lessons.

Unbeknownst to them, Irving Shapiro had been watching the encounter, his cupped hands near his face, pressing the bridge of his large nose against the studio window as the two engaged, and disappeared into the rear of the studio. He would keep this knowledge for a time when he could use it.

Chapter Eleven

Tom and Queenie were the only people in the Harrington home when Friday morning arrived. Tom wouldn't be there long–he and Max were going to East Lansing for a taste of college life, an evening frat house party at Michigan State. Queenie Harrington began preparing for her audition with Shapiro from the instant her feet went in her morning slippers. Brother and sister breezed past each other time and again while they rushed through the house gathering what each believed they needed. Neither knew what the other was planning, but both shared the frustration of watching the clock that seemed to contain a thousand hours on it, its hour hand moving painfully slow throughout the day.

 At three o'clock, they converged in the upstairs bathroom, both acting as though they were surprised the other was home.

 "Are you going somewhere?" Tom asked, noticing the three dresses his sister held draped over her forearm.

 Queenie had been practicing her story for a week, mentally getting it down so she could fly through her concocted ruse without stumbling. "Big plans, Tom. Charlotte Radke and I are double-dating tonight. Her cousin Elmer's in town from Germany. He's brought a friend with him, Hans, or something like that. They want to see a Tigers game at Navin Field." She tossed the dresses over a bathroom bench, acting out in nonchalant excitement. "What kind of name is Elmer? Sounds like a grumpy gramp's name. I'm supposed to pair up with him. I haven't met him yet, but I bet he's a bohunk. Charlotte said he's not, we'll see." The two stared at one another a moment, and she couldn't tell for certain if he believed her or not. So she changed the subject, and asked Tom what he had planned.

"Can you keep a secret?" her brother asked.

"Hell yes. Why?"

Tom found the opportunity to use some college lingo. "Well, Max and me are going to State for a frat drag, you know, a dance? And…you know Mother and Father, and what they'd say about that? I'd appreciate you keeping mum. Think you can do that? I won't say anything to them about the bullshit story you just laid on me, little sister."

Queenie stomped her heels in disappointment. "Oh come on. Wasn't I convincing enough? Tell me what I did wrong, I've been practicing that story for a week." Realizing she was without any heavy leverage against Tom, she asked, "Think they'll have any booze there at the party?"

"I'm sure we'll have the opportunity to imbibe, but you know me, I'm a good Catholic boy. I'd never violate my purity by getting a good jag on." Tom winked, and they laughed together.

"Bullshit baloney! I saw you and Max when you got into Father's Dewar's last Christmas, you were both canned," Queenie said, pushing Tom away from the bathroom doorway, taking first dibs of the room.

"I won't tell if you won't." Tom said, "It's going to be the bee's knees, Queenie. There'll be some fine chassis there, for sure. Max and me gotta be sure we don't get too edged. I don't want to hook up with some Bug-eyed Betty. We'll see. Now, what's your deal, the real deal?"

Queenie abandoned her ruse, actually relieved to be able to tell Tom the secret that had been bursting inside of her all week, confessing excitedly most everything that was going on that evening: the makeup and hair, photos, and then the big reveal on stage for an audition. The only bit she left out was Irving Shapiro.

"Who's putting all this together for you?"

Queenie stammered at the thought of telling Tom, but before she could say his name Tom said, "Those characters we met at the club?"

Queenie implored Tom, "Geezas, don't tell Mother and Father, please? Mr. Shapiro said I was going to be 'smash' downtown. He said I could hit it big, that people are going to love my singing. He's made a lot of stars out of young singers like me. That's what he said."

Tom dropped his hands to his sides and gave her a blank stare while he thought instinctively of the perils downtown posed to a young girl like his sister. And alone? "I don't like it, Queenie. Something about those two guys, they smelled like trouble. I still don't understand why they would show up at Shoepac without fishing gear, or even any luggage. They drove all that way just to get a look at the club? That's bushwa. What time is the audition? How are you getting there and back? Is anyone going to be with you, someone who can watch over you?"

Queenie, bowled over in excitement, made her case, but featuring another lie, "Oh, everything will work out fine. Charlotte is going with me, and you know her, she's very cautious. Mr. Shapiro is picking me…us up at Dolan's Diner on Woodward at five. He said he'd get me back home as soon as it's over, and that won't be too late." In a moment of frustration, she pleaded, "This is a big deal, Tom. I want you to be happy for me. It's the chance of a lifetime. I need you in on this, big brother." She studied Tom's weary look, waiting for a hint of acceptance. "Come on…"

"I can think of a thousand reasons for you not to go, but I know what you're feeling. I know that's your dream. Damn! I wish you had said something to me earlier. Maybe I could have gotten someone to go with you who could cover your back better than Charlotte Radke."

Tom hesitantly gave in but continued admonishing her when Max came to pick him up. "Break a leg!"

At four thirty, eighteen-year-old Charlotte Radke carefully chugged her father's brown-and-yellow Buick Roadster convertible up to curb in front of the Harrington house. She had been Max's intermittent girlfriend throughout high school, even though he found her to be too tame and unwilling to put out; she and Queenie, oddly, had hit it off. She wore her auburn hair combed back tightly beyond her freckled face, and tied it in place with a blue ribbon. Charlotte was a prig, and celibate as a nun. Queenie delighted in telling scandalous stories of her own escapades– some true–others invented. But Charlotte was only going to drive Queenie to Dolan's.

"Don't you look like a million bucks?" Charlotte exclaimed as Queenie sashayed through the doorway out to the curb, bedecked in a red dress with velvet caplets, a black squared yoke held in place with jeweled buttons on each shoulder.

"It's Mom's. Tell me what you think? Be honest." Queenie did a pirouette, her dress swirling at her ankles.

"The bee's knees, Queenie. You'll knock 'em out. Now, get in before you're late."

Charlotte let her off at the diner at ten to five. Both Queenie and Shapiro were relieved the other had showed up. Queenie felt Irving Shapiro appeared handsome in his stylish black suit, looking like a man of importance where he waited behind the diner inside his green Duesenberg Model J. When he saw her, he drove up to let her in.

"My God, Queenie, you look marvelous!" Shapiro remarked. "Are you ready for the big day?"

Queenie took her seat next to Shapiro and smoothed the folds of her dress across her lap. She took a breath and exhaled, "I'm getting the heebie-jeebies... Thank you."

"Don't thank me yet, we haven't accomplished anything so far. Everything will work out fine though– you'll be a smash. Oh, by the way, your name is Little Dove, and you're twenty-one."

"*Little Dove*? Okay. I think I'll like being twenty-one. Oh, I hope so," she said, undeterred and unfettered by the faux name. She fidgeted inside her purse. "You got a fag?"

Shapiro bumped a cigarette from his pack and passed it to her. She leaned toward the lighter in his hand while he lit hers and one for himself. "You'll only be Little Dove at the photographer's studio, okay? You'll be you on stage." He thought again. "Hell, I kinda' like Little Dove. What do you think?"

"Whatever it takes, whatever works. Sure...Little Dove."

Shapiro weaved impatiently through the Woodard Avenue traffic that clogged the street with other drivers like debris in a stream after a forceful rain, everyone rushing to begin their weekend away from work.

Spellman was waiting for them inside, camera loaded and ready, his portrait lights like a firing squad in the proximity of his gray-and-blue swirled-background.

Queenie and Shapiro entered. Queenie noticed Ruth Etting's portrait right off. "There she is," she hushed. "She's beautiful, my favorite!"

"Recognize her, do you?" Spellman asked, joining her at the photograph. "You must be Little Dove? The name fits you."

Queenie, remembering what Shapiro had told her, replied, "Yes, I'm Little Dove. I'm so pleased to be here. I hope I don't let you down."

"She was just starting out, too," Spellman said. "Notice her eyes? They're so sultry and took to my lights marvelously. You'll be fine, just leave everything to me, Miss Dove."

Queenie liked the sound of her new name: Miss Dove. Just then, two women approached from a small room down a narrow hallway and joined them. "This is Bambi, your makeup artist, and this is Mary, she'll be doing your hair."

In less than an hour, they completed Queenie's transformation and she was ready for Spellman's camera. Gone was her youthful teenage appearance. Mary had placed pin curls in her hair, which was now waved over one side of her round face. Queenie glowed like a warm, rubicund painting; her deep-blue eyes leaped forward like bright stars in a dark universe. Shapiro's lips separated when he saw her, stunned by her beauty.

Spellman seated Queenie and began posing her on a gold velvet chaise, with silver tufted buttons pillowing its backrest. She took to the posing as though this were her destiny. Spellman applied his techniques, titling her face just so to highlight her cheeks and eyes and hair. He continued posing and clicking the shutter of his camera beyond his routine photo sitting shots until Shapiro, jealously, said, "That's enough. We've got to go now."

Woodward Avenue was clogged with luxury cars lined up like folks in a ration line outside the Graystone Ballroom on both sides of the sun baked street in Detroit's Paradise Valley district. The concrete block building seemed to breathe and exhale steaming exhaust from the automobiles gathered outside. It was a typical scene for a Friday summer's night in downtown Detroit. Rumor had spread that Ben Selvin and his Band were making a guest appearance that evening, featuring a hotshot clarinet player named Benny Goodman. Jazz lovers from Detroit and Windsor, Ontario, were arriving early to grab a hard-to-get spot inside the grand ballroom. Queenie leaned out to look from her passenger window at the large gathering of uptown folks passing through the entrance below its brightly lit, vertical marquee. She felt a tightness taking hold in her stomach. She struggled to breathe, her mind beginning to doubt if she could perform.

Irving Shapiro drove past all the impatient honking and jaywalker attendees scooting across the bright avenue without concern. He rested his car at the alley's entrance where the musicians parked; he and the Feinsteins had a dubious ownership in the club, gaining them free license to bring whomever they wished to showcase on stage. The Feinstein gang had other privileges around Paradise Valley. They were treated well with certain perks because they provided the booze for many other venues.

Sensing Queenie's apprehension, he asked, "You look a little long in the tooth, are you alright?"

Queenie's face had turned pale. "I'll be fine, Mr. Shapiro. Maybe some water when we get inside. I'll be fine."

"Good, 'cause I'm getting you on stage with Selvin's band. He's coming in for a special performance tonight. It can't get any better than that for your introduction to the stage. The house will be packed."

Queenie sank further inside with the added pressure of singing with a world-renowned band. Small droplets of nervous moisture began to bead on her face, threatening to cause her rouge to deteriorate on her cheeks.

Shapiro brought her backstage and set her down on a stool before a pedestal fan. The breeze dried her makeup while the house orchestra began to play to the excited audience, the blur of its horns, piano, and drums thundering a din of indiscernible melody leaking backstage where she sat.

Shapiro stood behind the long, thick curtain that shielded the stage from where she was sitting. He called Queenie to join him to watch the throngs of people dancing and swinging in each other's arms while they moved frantically across the parquet flooring as Selvin's band played. Queenie walked slowly toward him. When she peered through the curtain's sliced opening, she began to feel faint with anxiety again. She went back to the stool, clutching her wet hands tightly across her lap.

"They're going to call you on stage any minute, but don't worry, I'll get you through this, trust me."

Queenie looked up at Shapiro; her eye makeup was melting away in watery streaks. "Help me. What do I do? I've waited for this moment forever, and I don't want to fail."

Shapiro now began to feel the pressure of Queenie's imminent failure. He had been touting Queenie's talent around town as a new singing diva who was going to shake the city with her incredible voice. He began to fear he was producing a dud that would make him look like a second-rate talent purveyor. "Damn it! Stay here, I'll be right back. Okay?" Shapiro assured her.

Shapiro walked quickly toward the darkest shadows of the backstage where Queenie couldn't see him. Two men, dressed in flashy suits, hovered over a dim candle flame, their faces brightened from the dancing candlelight. One of them held a spoon over the flame while the other waited for the lumpy powder in the spoon to liquefy, then he dipped the tip of a syringe into the bubbling spoon and sucked the heroin inside its barrel. Behind them, a muted overhead light showed only the outlines of their fedoras and shoulders. One was a drummer, the other a clarinet player, members of an all-black jazz band that played at the Graystone Ballroom on Mondays–the only time they were allowed to take the stage. They were there to listen to Selvin's orchestra but could do so only from backstage. The drummer removed his suit coat and rolled up his right sleeve. Shapiro joined them before the drug was injected.

"Hey, boys, hold on."

The drummer recognized Shapiro, and rushed to straighten his sleeve, embarrassed that he had been caught in his attempt to get high. "Evenin Mistah Shapiro, suh. How can I hep ya?"

"Before you do that" –he nodded to the syringe the other man was unable to hide "I want you to load this." Shapiro withdrew a worn leather pouch from his pocket that held a similar syringe and a small bag of heroin. He gave it to the drummer.

"Why, sha, Mistah Shapiro, anything for ya." The men repeated the melting process and then loaded the syringe, its chrome flaring under the dim lightbulb.

Shapiro removed his suit coat and rolled up his own sleeve. "Now tie it off and give it to me," he instructed.

The taller man tightened a strap above the hinge in Shapiro's arm to raise a vein and plunged the needle forward. Shapiro closed his eyes, welcoming the drug and the bliss it would bring.

He returned to Queenie at a much slower pace than he had left her. She was fraught with despair. Shapiro brought forth his leather pouch again, retrieving only the small bag of heroin. "Give me your hand, Queenie. This will help you to relax..."

Willing to try anything, Queenie presented her damp palm. He wiped away the warm perspiration with his handkerchief, gently blowing his breath across her skin to help it dry. He placed a pinch of powder in her open palm and said, "Lick this like it's sugar, and listen to the band play; it'll take your mind off your worries."

"What is this?"

"Medicine. It will relax you so much you'll think you're singing in heaven–closer than you'll probably ever get." Shapiro then took the flask of whiskey from his suit pocket. "Chase it down with a swig of this."

When Queenie bowed toward her palm, the pungent odor of vinegar came forth, causing her to pause. Shapiro reassured her, "It's okay, you'll be fine."

The powder immediately brought a tangy bitterness to her mouth, causing her face to cringe and her eyes to squint. She drank quickly from the flask, gulping twice, trying to displace the foul taste in her mouth. "That's some nasty shit, Irving. Are you sure it'll work?

Shapiro gutted a pinched laugh. "You'll see in a few minutes. Remember, it's medicine."

Queenie closed her eyes and began humming a dead song from her past, waiting for the "medicine" to displace her fears. Minutes later, as though the heroin were waiting for a time clock to punch in, her mouth and eyes began shaping into a dreamy smile.

The orchestra stopped playing, and the audience hushed. A voice spoke to the microphone saying there was a special guest making her debut performance. The voice called out, "Little Dove, would you come out here?"

Queenie rose from the stool, her shoes dropped silently against the floor. She felt like a leaf drifting on a slow stream as she walked past Shapiro as he separated the curtain for her to enter the stage. A bright spotlight wrapped over her and she felt its warmth; the waves of her hair glistened like moonlight illuminating a ghost from a different world. She stepped to the microphone. The audience sat like a congregation in church to hear a sermon from the altar. Ribbons of blue-and-gold patterns swirled elegantly toward the domed ceiling, and its fresco paintings. The low voices collected and rose high above the dance floor, a hush not unlike murmurings from pious visitors to a chapel meant for a deity. Rows of folks were seated in the balcony that encircled the immense room, eagerly awaiting the voice of the new singer. They leaned forward in their chairs, pausing to pass judgment on this unknown songstress.

Queenie craned her head to the bandmaster and whispered the song she would like to sing, "Someone to Watch Over Me in D…" The guitarist thumbed a string on his guitar for Queenie to find her reference. The orchestra began.

When Queenie sang the last stanza, and the band finished the song, the audience sat motionless, quietly deciphering what they had just heard. As though a door had opened, and a rush of wind had returned their voices, the audience erupted in ecstatic cheering and clapping. Queenie stood at the microphone and bowed. The cheering continued. She bowed again. A man rushed to the stage with a bouquet of roses, tossing them at her feet.

The blinding spotlight faded when Queenie floated past the curtain to return to its dark beginning. Shapiro retrieved the roses and gave them to Queenie. "See…I knew they'd love you. Get ready to be a star, Queenie."

"I'm in heaven," Queenie said, bathed in her ephemeral moment of grace.

Shapiro handed her a glass of champagne. Queenie drank quickly, and returned the glass for a refill.

Shapiro took her by the hand to lead her past the adoring staff that had collected behind stage, clapping and smiling at the new star. "I could listen to you sing that song forever. That will be our song, Little Dove, 'Someone to Watch Over Me.'

"I'll sing it for you anytime, Irving." She rested her empty glass on a stool, and asked, "Can I have some more heaven?"

"Too soon for that, Little Dove. It can wait."

Hell would be waiting its turn.

Chapter Twelve

Queenie didn't go home that night. Instead, Shapiro took her on a voyage of ill-begotten intention, an expedition through his world of conquest and seduction, filling her with destructive concoctions that lasted throughout the night. He brought her back to Birmingham just as the sun was rising.

Queenie sulked in the seat beside him, not considering the awakening of the shops and businesses coming back to life for another day of commerce along Woodward Avenue. A flower shop merchant was watering his display of plants and flowers on the sidewalk in front of his store. He waved the soaker wand over the flora, and looked and nodded at them as they drove by. Queenie's response was an empty stare.

She was being dropped off as though she were a pedestrian riding in a taxi. She was still groggy from the alcohol and heroin. Her body ached. She knew she had done something physical during the night with Shapiro. She remembered her performance on stage, but the lingering pain she felt between her legs told her she had been performing something else for the first time. Slowly, the jagged memory came forward, and she closed her eyes.

"Are you up for breakfast?" Shapiro asked.

Queenie considered the question during a long pause. "No, I'm not hungry. I just want to be home, get some sleep."

Shapiro tapped his open hand on her lap as though he was petting the wither of a tired horse. Queenie had no response.

When he steered into the Harringtons' driveway, the neighborhood was still at rest, except for a smattering of kitchen lights where early risers were perking morning coffee. Queenie unlatched the car door to depart. With the door ajar, she asked, "What happens now?"

"I'm leaving town for a few days. Call me during the week, and I'll tell you what's lined up, where you will perform next. Okay?"

Queenie brightened. "I made it, I got the job?"

"Queenie, you've had the job all along. Congratulations. I told you before, everything would fall in place," Shapiro said, lulling his eyes in reassurance.

Queenie began to step from the car. "Hey, wait! Don't forget this," Shapiro said, extending his arm and folded hand that held a fifty-dollar bill. "You're a professional now. Pros get paid."

Queenie took the money, and then walked away to enter the house from a side door at the driveway, regarding the fifty like it was a prize for taking the hardest punch a body could take.

****

Sunday morning, Irving Shapiro drove north with a heavy mind on Highway 23 in his Duesenberg Model J. His connection to the Feinsteins was at a point where he felt he could do better on his own. He plotted how he was going to make his break from him, but first he had to deal with the Skipper and Chief Louie's betrayal. He spoke to the empty space within his automobile, to the concrete road din, as if it would return an answer. He craned his head to the back seat where his tommy gun was packed in its case. *Did Skipper swipe the booze, or did the chief? Skipper was doing all right himself before we came along…But no, it can't be the Skipper. We set him up pretty good with the money he'd make. No, he wouldn't jeopardize a long-term deal. Now, the chief. I don't know him from Abraham. Maybe one of his men? Could Skipper and the chief be working together on this?* He mulled the possibilities as best he could while his mind kept trying to relive the young luscious body of Queenie underneath him just hours earlier. The memory made it difficult to concentrate. Eventually he concluded, *Too many spoons in the soup. Only way to get the right guy is to kill 'em all.* He laughed nervously after considering Frank Feinstein's certain disapproval of losing their hard-to-come-by importing arrangement, but Feinstein was expendable, too.

Shapiro took Highway 23 until he came to Lachine. He slowed his Duesenberg to allow a horse-drawn flatbed wagon, filled with flats of fresh strawberries, to cross the highway. A young farm boy holding the reins tipped his Stormy Kromer hat to Shapiro, thanking him for the courtesy. Shapiro nodded and continued toward Posen where the hardwood hills changed to groomed, furrowed potato fields that baked in the unimpeded afternoon sun. He was less than an hour away from Rogers City.

Miss Silly sloshed the head of her wet brush across a bay window of the International Hotel, and didn't pay any mind to Shapiro's Duesenberg when it slowed to a stop behind her. When the car door thumped shut, she turned his way, recognizing him immediately.

"Howdy, Mr. West. How's tricks?" She grinned, puffing a breath of air toward the displaced hair strung over her eyes.

"I'm here to see Skipper, is he about?" he asked pleasantly, avoiding any sign of his true demeanor and intentions.

Miss Silly cupped her hands around her temples, and pressed her face to the wet window to see the clock inside the lobby. "He's probably just mooring the *Madame* right now down at Seagull Point, and loadin' today's catch in his pickup. He should be by shortly." She rewet her brush in a soapy pail, and went over the drying window again. "Mind if I drag a squeegee across this window before it dries again?"

Shapiro had returned to his car without responding; he knew how to get to Seagull Point. He set out to find the Skipper.

The *Madame* came to view when he drove through the passage of sandy knolls and horsetail reeds leading to the cove. Skipper's flatbed truck was backed against the dock's approach. Skipper was pouring ice in the deep containers of whitefish he had removed from the nets, their silver backs shimmering, sparkling below the ice. Sandpipers scurried nervously over the beach sand hoping to share the catch while patient gulls swirled on the overhead wind currents, waiting to follow Skipper's truck back to his shack where he would begin filleting them.

Shapiro sat the Duesenberg beside the flatbed truck, and stood in the damp sand behind his opened door, his pistol holstered in plain view, strapped to his chest. Skipper halted his work when he saw the Duesenberg. He saw the pistol.

"Ay, Mr. Shapiro, what brings you this way? A friendly visit?" Skipper asked, dispensing the ice more slowly, like a mailman approaching a house where a vicious dog was chained. How long was its chain? "I'm not due to make a pickup until tomorrow morning… Is everything okay?"

Shapiro closed the car's door and walked over slowly, in no hurry, to the Skipper. "You've got a big problem, Skipper. The last delivery was watered down. I'm here to find out how that happened. You got any answers?"

Skipper stepped from the dock hesitantly. "I don't know how that can be. I checked a couple cases myself…the bottles were perfect."

"You should have checked more carefully, half of the booze was cut. Some greedy son of a bitch helped himself to half of our stuff. Tell me how that happened?"

Shapiro analyzed Skipper's meek and innocent reaction. *Is he telling the truth? Is he a wolf in sheep's clothes?* came into thought while Skipper dodged any involvement in the swindle. He knew a man like Skipper surely had learned the ropes in life having sailed around the world, witnessed by the long list of fading tattoos inked on his forearms. *Has he killed anyone? If he had the chance, would he kill me?* added to his thoughts.

"I swear I had nothing to do with this, Mr. Shapiro," Skipper pleaded, holding his palms open at his waist. But he knew it had to be Louie the Thief and his Anishinaabe crew. He knew Shapiro was going to kill someone because of it. "It had to be someone on the other side." He turned, nodding to the north across the big lake.

"We're going for a ride, Skipper."

"Where to?"

Shapiro nodded in the same direction.

"What about my catch? It'll spoil if I don't get it back to the hotel."

"You better get Miss Silly to come get it, because you're going for a cruise, right now. Fire up the *Madame*."

Skipper dragged his hand across his forehead and removed his hat. "Can I drive it back to the hotel? There's no phone out here."

Shapiro palmed the grip of his .45 in its holster. "Fuck the fish! Let's go."

Skipper got aboard his fish tug and lit the engine. He hoisted a yellow flag of warning on his bow staff without Shapiro noticing. It was a flag showing disease on board. Shapiro attended to the assembly of his tommy gun.

They set off for the Les Cheneaux Islands where they would search for Louie the Thief.

Shapiro braced against a peeled-paint bulkhead of the small pilot house, cradling his tommy gun, watching the Skipper maneuver through the rolling waves.

Skipper's mind raced as he considered the few opportunities he'd have to confront Shapiro. He looked about the wheelhouse, searching for a weapon he could use to engage Shapiro when the time was right. Hanging from the bulkhead was a gaff hook and line he used when a large sturgeon was netted. *I'll keelhaul that kike sonofabitch when he least expects it.* It was five miles out in the Straits before Skipper spoke.

"There's a chance Louie could be in St. Ignace, ya know. It'll be dark before we could get there from Les Cheneaux."

Shapiro considered the possibility. "I think not. I'm willing to bet he's with the booze, and that's at the usual pickup spot, right?"

"Yeah, it should be on the island."

"Just keep it on course for the islands, Skipper."

The *Madame* entered the wide channel between Little LaSalle and Marquette Islands, plowing forward to Duck Bay where Louie and his Anishinaabe men held the whiskey. The waters calmed away from the big lake. The only sounds were the murmur of the diesel, and the purr of water rolling away from its hull.

Duck Bay revealed itself like an empty dinner plate, its surface still and placid, nuzzled below spiraling conifers that bowed toward her lee shore. A dark man scurried along the rocky shore toward the dock where Skipper always loaded the whiskey, meeting them as the *Madame* coasted to the dock pilings to receive the tie line from Skipper. On the opposite side of the dock was moored another vessel, similar in size to Skipper's fish tug. Several of Louie's men were off-loading cases of whiskey, bringing them to shore. The *Madame's* yellow flag flittered above the forward deck. Chief Louie saw the flag, and buckled a pistol holster around his waist while several of his alerted workers hurried to replace the lids on the opened cases of whiskey. A wooden barrel filled with lake water sat near the whiskey.

Skipper waited for Louie to speak.

"*Boozhoo. Gdizhichge na?*" Louie asked of the yellow flag of disease, and the stranger he had on board the *Madame*.

"*En', en'*, the bees are gone," Skipper replied in the same language.

"I don't know what you just said, but shut your pie hole!" ordered Shapiro.

Louie and his men stood behind the scattered whiskey cases, defiant, caught in their thievery, their dark eyes wide with anticipation, their feet driven in the pebble landscape as though the earth would assist them. Beside him stood the captain of the other vessel. Louie said, "I know what you're thinking, *niijkiwisag*. This is not how it appears. Why, this whiskey belongs to another client," Louie explained with an unbelievable yarn. "Your whiskey has not arrived yet. Is this not correct, *Ozaawaa-bneshiinh*?" he asked the captain of the other boat, who was slowly stepping away from his close proximity to Louie.

"Yes, this must be so," The captain replied unconvincingly.

"*Gonif!*" Shapiro shouted, calling Louie a thief. "You and your men are momzers, liars!" Shapiro moved quickly past Skipper to a position on the dock. Louie grasped at his pistol, but before he could unholster it, Shapiro raised the machine gun waist high, and pulled the trigger in short bursts until Louie and his men fell to the limestone and pebble ground without a cry or word. He then turned his aim toward the captain, who was frozen in his stance, wondering if he was going to be shot down, too.

Shapiro asked the captain in a calm, nonchalant voice, "Are you a businessman? What's your name?"

The Anishinaabe captain hesitated in shock, and replied, "Yellow Bird, but I seem to be unemployed at the present time, sir."

"Would you be interested in a private business arrangement with me, running whiskey to Cheboygan twice a month, starting now?"

"I am now, that's the best offer I've had all day, sir. I can have fifty cases to you same time next week. Cheboygan, you say?"

"Yes, Duncan Bay. There'll be someone waiting for you and that old scow over there."

The captain lowered his raised hands and gave Skipper an apologetic look, knowing what was in store for him.

Shapiro turned to Skipper, who was holding his hands above his head, his face haggard in fear.

"What are you waiting for?" Shapiro said.

"Get it over with!" Skipper said, closing his eyes as though it would lessen the shock of his death.

"Start loading the whiskey."

****

Somewhere between the Les Cheneaux Islands and Duncan Bay, where there was no demarcation, or waypoint, or landmark, a vessel the size of the *Madame* cruised urgently toward them at full power. The bow of the craft cut the lake water in heavy furls that shoveled a bubbling after path in its wake. Skipper vised the helm of the *Madame* as though he expected water to drip from the raised tendons rippling across the tops of his hands.

The vessels tied together in the midmost region of the big lake. The sun made slanting gray shadows of their twin outlines on the jiggered water.

Once again, Skipper took to the task of carrying the cases of whiskey, off-loading it to the other boat.

When the last case was placed, Shapiro stood in the *Madame's* cabin with Skipper. "You couldn't stand success, could you?"

Skipper was silent, plotting how he would make his play to survive; his life had run out of time. Shapiro lifted the tommy gun, pointing it at him. Skipper made his move, suddenly slamming the throttle forward and then back, jerking the wheel left and right, violently snapping the bowline and rocking the two vessels, causing Shapiro to slam against a bulkhead. Skipper rushed for the gaff hook and gripped it with both hands. Shapiro tried to re-steady himself and the tommy gun. Skipper swung the gaff hook wildly at him, catching his shoulder where the hook sunk in. He yanked on the rope to set the hook deeper into Shapiro's flesh, causing him to cry out in agony while Skipper pulled him toward the open deck where he could dump him below the deep water. Shapiro fought to get a foothold, finally bracing himself against the bulkhead. Finding his footing,

Shapiro got control of his tommy gun and began blurting errantly aimed shots at Skipper, who had released the gaff line and dove headfirst into the lake.

The other boat returned to the *Madame*, pulling up closely so Shapiro could get aboard. The riled water between the boats showed red swirls of blood that blended within its blue shade. He knew then that he had struck Skipper with at least one round. A frightened deckhand gawked at the gaff hook embedded in Shapiro's shoulder and the blood oozing profusely below the hook. "Don't just stand there, pull the Goddamn thing out!" With his good arm, he emptied his tommy gun, riddling the *Madame* relentlessly with every round in the its magazine.

Hovering above, gulls jettisoned away from the craft on a sudden up drafting current, and the tommy gun's calamity, dismissing the air beneath them with a series of labored wing motions.

It took hours before the fish tug sank to the bottom of the Straits of Mackinac.

Chapter Thirteen

Irving Shapiro kept his ambiguous promise to Queenie Harrington. He brought her to lesser-known downtown clubs to perform, explaining, "You'll need to cut your teeth on smaller crowds and gain some stage knowledge before I get you on the big stage again." This went on for months without the Harringtons knowing. She told them she had an evening job at J. L. Hudson department store, downtown on Woodward Avenue, working in the cosmetic section. Shapiro arranged for her to be picked up at Dolan's Diner on the weekends she was to perform. When the clubs closed, she was taken home in the early hours of each forgettable sunrise. She would sleep all day to recover from her heroin and alcohol intoxication, masking its odor by spritzing herself with pungent perfume. She became an exceptionally good liar.

****

Shapiro kept with his plan as Queenie progressed, and her act became well polished; he booked her into some of the city's most prestigious nightclubs where the name "Little Dove" appeared in bright, flashing lights on each marquee. He took her on elaborate shopping sprees, so she would be dressed in the finest evening wear that was fitting for a stage star. Little Dove's splendid performances caused her star to rise suddenly in popularity within the nightclub scene. Folks began noticing her and seeking out her scheduled performances, begging for autographs when she arrived at the clubs while Shapiro arrogantly paraded her through the audience as though she was a thoroughbred racehorse prancing proudly about a paddock. They fawned over her with gushing compliments and admiration for the indelible talent she possessed.

But her stardom was beginning to unwind like a fragile seam within the realm of Shapiro's ulterior guidance. Her fondness, then dependence to alcohol and heroin grew, and graduated from a few glasses of champagne and a lick of her palm to straight heroin injection before and after each performance. The only behavior that diminished was her ability to say no to him, and her frail, impressionable principles. She couldn't say no while he zealously seduced her, either. He was obsessed with her young body, her naiveté that excited him as though he were robbing a bank without being caught. But that began to wane, too. She no longer protested his sexual advances, the very thing that he found thrilling when he charged within her. Instead, she began acquiescing to indifference and servitude, lying lifelessly while he went about his business.

Eventually, her family became suspicious of her secret weekend life, her recalcitrant attitude when refusing to attend family affairs, her unwillingness to discuss her job—any interrogatory relating to the long weekend absences that had become predictably routine.

Soon the cost of her heroin use exceeded the pay she received from performing. Shapiro made her a slave to her addiction. The family crisis reached a boiling point on Queenie's seventeenth birthday when she had exhausted every believable explanation she could invent for her parents' and her brothers' appeasement. The pressure became overwhelming, so she moved out. She told them she wished to be on her own, and to leave her alone in her decision. There were times she called to tell them she was fine, but she really wasn't. There was little they could do when she told them to leave her unfound.

Shapiro put Queenie in a seedy hotel in the midst of a bleak Detroit winter, where others like her succumbed to their addiction beneath the hideous furnishings, among the pleadings of vulgar voices, and blanketed by obnoxious odors that insulted the senses of visitors to his brothel on Hastings Street. He used her body to perform for his clients and himself in order to pay her debt that he made sure she could never climb above.

He kept her sober enough to perform on the weekends, and because of her youth, her body withstood the assault of the drugs longer than most, but she couldn't keep from slipping forever further into a masochistic world of cravings, and the despicable acts she performed to get what she had once called heaven.

Inevitably, her health began to fail on her inescapable voyage to perdition. With each injection, the brightness and vigor of her youth slowly leached away, drained and replaced by a haggard and hollow dullness, her skin like the petals of a poisoned flower. This now was her life.

****

April 1931 came. Spring. Hastings Street was slushed from a mild snow, its sidewalks and curbs holding the dregs of human consumption in an ugly collection of cigarette butts, discarded wrappers, and oily stains from automobile discharges that left rainbow-colored streams limping into its gutters.

Shapiro smelled vomit as he entered Queenie's room. The early-morning light tracked through a jaundice-colored curtain, leaving bright patches on the dusty hardwood floor. He couldn't see Queenie but heard her gasping. He stepped farther into the room where he saw her kneeling with her arms draped around the toilet, expelling the sour bile from her stomach. She knew it was him but didn't acknowledge his entrance. He quickly changed his lustful intentions at the sight of her unattractive pose, and stench. Three ten-dollar bills lay on a nightstand close to an unkempt bed, its sheet revealing a stain from her previous evening's work. Shapiro clutched the bills and put them in his vest pocket.

"I see our client was by last night. Where's the rest of it? There's supposed to be fifty. Are you having a sale on fucking, or something? Which one was he?

Someone has to come up with the rest of the dough," he demanded.

Queenie rose from the floor and stirred a towel over her wet chin. "I don't remember. Joe Shit the Ragman, I guess? Who cares, he said it was only worth thirty bucks." She wobbled into the open room where Shapiro was standing near the window, spreading the curtain to view the contents of Hastings Street where his Duesenberg was parked below. He withdrew a worn leather pouch from his overcoat and opened it. He removed the syringe from its place in the folder. "Do you want a fix this morning?"

Queenie found the corner of the bed and sat with her knees spread, resting her head between her palms, her elbows braced on her knees. "What do you think?" she said, her voice crass and cold, a stranger's voice.

Shapiro removed his overcoat and placed it on a wooden chair near the window. "You know how it is. This first." He approached the bed, unbuckled his belt, and let his trousers crowd over his shoes.

Queenie completed her bargain with Shapiro, but he withheld his contribution. "You'll get this when the rest of the money shows up."

Queenie sprung from the bed, furious. "I wasn't told it would be fifty. Goddammit! Why are you fucking around with me?"

Shapiro fastened his buckle and adjusted his twisted vest. "You ungrateful bitch!" he screamed. He swept his hand over his shoulder with swift force, striking Queenie across her temple. Queenie fell onto the bed, weeping, curling her body in a fetal contraction of submission.

"Please, I'm begging you. I need it, Irving. Don't take it from me," she pleaded, her face swollen where his palm had struck her. "Please…"

Shapiro returned the syringe to its holder, and folded his overcoat across his arm. He reached for Queenie, jerking her forcibly from the bed. "Let me show you what happens when someone crosses me." He dragged her from the room and down the hallway to a similar room where Bunny, another of his "girls," was roomed. From the hallway, she could hear the moans and whimpering of Bunny, who was suffering from acute drug withdrawal and Mo Rueben. Shapiro was punishing her because she told him she wanted to get clean and leave his employment, something that was forbidden by him. Bunny had been skimming money from her evenings' work, too, so she'd have some dough when she bolted to freedom. Shapiro knew the money was somewhere in her possession.

They entered Bunny's room. The scant furniture was lying skewed, tossed about on the floor. Dresser drawers were pillaged with clothes strewn everywhere. Mo Rueben, Shapiro's discipline specialist, was standing over Bunny, who was naked and shackled to the bedposts by leather straps as though she were a beaver pelt. Rueben was known downtown as a madman who was a specialist in the way he tortured his victims. He was in charge of keeping Shapiro's women in line, keeping them in the fold. His forte was inventing despicable techniques of vaginal disfigurement. In his last act of cruelty, he'd gathered a group of Shapiro's women together to witness him pouring boiling water from a teapot onto the vagina of a call girl who had planned to quit her job, permanently disfiguring her.

   A tall candle burned on a nightstand beside Bunny, its wax melted away to expose a long wick and flame. Rueben was holding a sulfur sparkler in one hand, the kind kids used on Independence Day, and several spent sparklers were lying on the floor. He began waving the unlit sparkler above the candle's flame until its tip flashed brightly. Bunny's bindings were cinched so tightly around her wrists and ankles that the leather couldn't be seen below the swelling. Her face was as pale as a corpse, except for his fist imprints on her forehead and a stream of blood coming from a gash on her bulging lower lip. Her torso revealed red, blistering welts from her breast to her thighs. Rueben was robed in a black apron that showed splotches of Bonny's vomit and blood. It was tied snuggly around his portly stomach to protect his clothing. If the apron were white, he would have passed for a butcher. Rueben's physical efforts came with heavy breathing and guttural grunts while Bunny resisted, but to no avail—she was too weakened from the beatings and the two days she had gone without heroin. She was now begging for the loaded syringe lying on the nightstand close to the candle, but she still hadn't turned over the money. To her, the syringe seemed a million miles away, but the ignited sparkler represented a painful, immediate reality. Rueben's face was glossed with sweat that was leaching into his dark hairline. He giggled at her sight, like he was an adolescent child, followed by his three-pack-a-day smoker's cough. He was so taken up with his torturing process of holding a lighted sparkler close to her torso that he paid no notice to Shapiro and Queenie when they entered.

Bunny pleaded, her voice gurgling from her blood-filled mouth. She swung her head toward the syringe on the nightstand. "I was wrong… I'll give it back, I need you…I'll do anything, just give me some…a little taste, maybe. Hey, how about I give ya a good suck job? Please…"

Rueben's face brightened. He had accomplished his goal of reducing Bunny's will to zero. Lifting the syringe from the table and removing the needle from its barrel, he said, "Sure, I'll give you some sweet stuff now, little cunt, but first you have to give me the money."

Bunny could hold out no longer, confessing its location. "It's down there…" She nodded toward her womanhood.

"I figured that's where you were hiding it, but that would have been too easy. I wouldn't have had any fun before you confessed." Rueben thrust his hand inside her vagina and pulled out the tightly rolled bills.

"Okay, you've got it. What about…"

"Yup, a deal is a deal." He pressed his palm over her nose and mouth, leaving just the meaty flesh of her torn lip exposed. The sparkler continued to burn after he shoved it into her vagina. While Bunny writhed violently, he kept his end of the deal and rammed the blunt syringe into the exposed flesh of her lip and pushed the plunger. Bunny's screams were muted by his hand. She thrashed against her bindings. Finally, her bloodshot eyes focused on Shapiro, who was wincing at the sight of Rueben's debauchery. Queenie slumped and hugged the wall as though it would give her refuge, but Shapiro yanked her upright, making sure she got a clear message of what awaited her should she cross him. He guided her back to her room.

"I'll be back this afternoon. You better come up with the rest of the money, or Mr. Rueben will pay you a visit and you'll get some heaven. Have a wonderful day, you little cunt."

Shapiro's leather soles whispered atop the hardwood floor as he walked toward the door. Queenie took some measure to compose herself, rising from the bed to gather her clothes. By the time she'd pulled her dress over her head, she could hear Shapiro's car door open and slam closed. He drove away into the mix of Saturday traffic on Hastings Street.

Queenie removed a pillow from its case, and used it as a bindle to carry her belongings. There wasn't much. She left behind the fancy dresses he had bought her for the stage. She took only what she had when she left home, the pearls from her grandmother, a few pairs of shoes, and her possibles. She draped the pearls over her small, now bony shoulders.

When she stepped onto the Hastings Street sidewalk, her low-cut shoes sank into the melting slush above her ankles. The briny mix of salt and snow made her soles slip around, and the slush numbed her ankles. She struggled to walk but continued up Hastings Street until she was able to stop a cab.

"Where to, miss?" the young driver asked, bumping a brown fedora higher on his forehead with his fingertips. The name, Lenny, was handwritten on a small card propped on the dashboard. Seeing the lowly condition Queenie was fraught with, the driver cringed apologetically, but asked suspiciously, "You got the dough for the ride?"

Queenie removed the pearls from her neck, and replied, "This should cover the fare, Lenny."

Lenny laced the pearls through his fingers, examining them closely. "You bet they will. Now, where did you say you want to go?"

"Straight up Woodward to Birmingham. You know where that is?"

"I'll find it," he said, balling the long necklace into his coat pocket.

When she arrived at her parents' home in Birmingham, she struck the brass ring against the strike plate on the oak door entrance, then squeezed the door lever to open it, undecided whether she was a visitor or a family member. Her father approached to answer the knock. Queenie fell into his arms, defeated and broken.

He held her while she wept, bringing her to a gold-trimmed sofa where she collapsed from exhaustion. Helen Harrington heard her sobbing, and came from the kitchen. She knelt beside Queenie and stroked the loose bangs away from her eyes. "You're home now, my darling. Everything will be fine from here on."

When they removed her overcoat, her brutal history could be read like dots on a road map of recent puncture marks, battle scars along the length of her forearms. The corners of her lips showed ruddy and oozing blisters.

The many months of searching for Queenie were finally over. Tom, ladened with guilt for not preventing her from going on that fateful audition, made frequent trips home to help with the family's exhaustive quest of finding her that began by them looking for the name "Queenie" on first-class venue marquees and, finally, smoke-filled speakeasies where the poorer folks sought refuge in bathtub gin and undefinable alcoholic concoctions. Shapiro had planned well by disguising her with the name Little Dove.

Helen took Queenie upstairs where she bathed her, and then helped her into her bed, but Queenie couldn't sleep. She writhed below the cotton bedcovering, caught in the height of pain from needing to be fixed. Doctor Harrington fetched his black bag. He shook a small vial and guided the sharp tip on a syringe past the seal, holding it above his eyes, watching the contents being sucked inside its glass barrel. He gently pierced the hinge in her arm, slowly plunging the drug inside a vein.

Queenie stilled beneath the bedcovering. A thin smile straightened her lips, the first one in a long time. She fell to sleep.

Chapter Fourteen

Tom Harrington and Max Milton came home for spring break that first year at Michigan State, on a Friday evening, the second week of April. They had two weeks off. Max wanted to go with Tom to the club to fish with Ike Powers, but he decided to give Charlotte Radke one more chance in hopes of deflowering her. Tom's brother, John Harrington, was in Singapore studying ancient religion with a selected group of university students. The Harringtons received letters and postcards regularly from John that always began with "namaste." He told them he was well and thankful for the opportunity to broaden his mind through The Four Noble Truths doctrine through "dhyana," a Buddhist form of deep concentration. In his last correspondence, he said he wouldn't return until midsummer. His family worried and wondered if he ever would return at all, given his proclivity for esoteric knowledge.

The Detroit weather was mild. The warm rains greened the lawns, and the sounds of baseballs popping into leather gloves could be heard in every neighborhood, but a spring snow storm had struck in Presque Isle County. A heavy frost came with it and killed the apple and cherry blossoms on their branches. There would be few trees able to bear fruit the coming summer. But the forecast was for better weather to come where Tom could get on Shoepac Lake and fish.

The Runners

Tom tossed his laundry bags in the hallway and went upstairs. He heard his parents talking with Queenie. He was relieved she was home, but he knew how bad off she was. When he entered the room, Queenie was beneath the covers suffering from withdrawal. The small dosages of morphine Doctor Harrington was giving her only kept her demons marginally satisfied. She tried to rest, but she was still gripped by the pain that comes with not getting her drug.

Tom sat at the edge of her bed. Queenie's eyes moistened when she regarded Tom with a pathetic look of, "I'm in trouble–I need your help." He placed his hand on hers and began to cry remorsefully. They didn't speak for ta long moment.

"It isn't over yet, Tom. He'll come for me, I just know he will. He's a madman. I was a money maker for him and he won't let that go without some sort of payoff that benefits him." She brushed her tears away. "I'm scared to death what he'll want and what he'll do to get it."

Tom squeezed her hand and left the bedroom to join their parents in the kitchen. Queenie asked him not to leave. He said he would come back soon.

Helen poured fresh coffee for Tom, remaining quiet while Doctor Harrington read from a medical journal. There was something more to be told about Queenie's condition.

"Is there something else going on that I'm not aware of, Father?" Tom asked.

Doctor Harrington placed a page marker in the journal and folded it. "She's about two months pregnant, Tom. I'm worried about her condition…I'm only giving her a small douse of morphine, and it will only alleviate her cravings for a short time. To give her more could harm the fetus. I'm afraid she'll have to deal with the agony without the help of drugs."

Tom held his cup with both hands, cradling its warmth like he was holding a small bird. He pondered what he was learning about his little sister's health. He had no answers but thought of an action that would presently satisfy him. Tom gripped his cup tightly. "I could kill that sonovabitch for doing this to her! What did she mean when she said Shapiro wouldn't let her go?" he asked.

"I can only imagine what she meant," Helen said, "and it sickens me." She went silent as her mind conjured images of what her daughter had been forced to do, and began to cry.

"There's more," Doctor Harrington said, his tone wary with warning. "I wouldn't be surprised if she has other ailments we are not aware of that have yet to show themselves." With that, he returned purposely to his medical journal.

Helen became inconsolable. She wept openly, her hands cradling her face against the kitchen table. Her usual stoic barrier now infiltrated by the feeling of hopelessness for little Queenie.

The Harringtons stayed at the table for hours, caught in exhausting thoughts of what to do next. Should they resist or retreat from the impending threat and danger that surely was coming from Shapiro?

"I wish John was back from Asia. Maybe he could advise us how Buddha could help?" Helen lamented in a moment of lightheartedness.

Tom replied, "I'd rather have Ike Powers's help right now, Mother."

Helen dabbed tears away. "I want my family together right now."

The family returned to Queenie each time she called out for one of them from her upstairs room, begging each to stay with her. During her intermittent dozing, they would convene to the kitchen only to be summoned again in short time.

Doctor Harrington knew she needed immediate medical help, and she should be admitted to Beaumont where he could get the best of care for her. They concluded this would be their best plan. He made several phone calls to the hospital. She would be admitted the following day. Helen Harrington sat in a chair beside Queenie until she fell asleep.

During the early hours beyond midnight, a car drove into the Harringtons' driveway, its motor idling while it sat next to the side-door entrance. It was Irving Shapiro and his bent-nosed accomplice, Mo Rueben.

Queenie was not sleeping. Her senses were acutely tuned to every sound and motion around her. She could hear the low rumble of the idling car outside. Her family was asleep, and not aware of the car in the driveway. She knew what was at hand, she knew it would be Shapiro coming for her. Folding the bedcovers from her body, she found her way through the dark hallway to the window above the side entrance. Below, she saw Shapiro's car boiling exhaust, gathering in a gray cloud in the faint light. Tom's bedroom was two doors away. She thought of waking him but feared Shapiro would do him harm if he went outside to confront them. Instead, she slowly made her way down the stairs to the side entrance. She would confront him on her own, perhaps convince him to finally leave her alone. She tripped the side door light, and its yellow incandescent glow fell on the car where Shapiro's cigarette smoldered faintly between his fingers. He sat behind the wheel and puffed his cigarette, blowing a swirling cloud that escaped through the opened car window. He saw Queenie slip through the doorway. She stood near the car in her bathrobe, steadying herself with one hand braced on the fender. Shapiro stepped into the yellow light, dragging one last time on his cigarette before flicking it to the ground where it sparked in a sudden short-lived flash.

"Hello, Little Dove. I knew you'd come," Shapiro said, stepping closer to Queenie.

"Please go, Irving. I will never go back to that life. You have to leave me alone now. If my parents see you here, they'll call the police." Queenie's voice sounded shallow and weak in her own ears.

Shapiro withdrew his leather pouch from his pocket and held it up in front of Queenie, tempting her. Queenie stared at the pouch; she was drowning in agony, submerged between her desire for the drug that would be like medicine for her now and her resilience to get clear of it. She chose to hold her breath and suffer. "No, I won't!"

Shapiro saw her resolve. He summoned Rueben from the car. "I think you will. You've met my associate, Mr. Rueben, remember him? You've seen his special talents."

Rueben moved from the car to join them in the driveway. He tipped his hat with a metal object he held in his hand. He said in a low voice, "So you're Miss Queenie? Mr. Shapiro says we've met, but I don't remember—I must have been busy then." Rueben coughed a sarcastic laugh and gave her an up-and-down look, as though he were inspecting a farm animal. "Tasty. I've heard a lot about you. I know you've heard of me."

Queenie shrank in fear, stepping back from his proximity. "Don't do this, Irving. This doesn't have to happen."

"Oh, you are so correct, Queenie. This doesn't have to happen at all. All you need to do is get in the car, and we'll go back…home," Shapiro said, and he almost sounded gentle and caring, until his breathing began to quicken in anger.

"I can't do that. I won't do that," Queenie said. She found some strength in thinking of how Shapiro had lied to her, how he had used her to his benefit. She began to feel rage building toward him. "You are a lying mother fucker, Shapiro! You promised me anything you could think of to get me to follow you. And, what has happened? Look what you've done to me! I'm a Goddamn drug addict and a whore because of you. A year ago, I was just a teenage girl! You'll rot in hell for doing this to me and all of the other girls down there."

Shapiro nodded to Rueben, who moved quickly to Queenie, pinning her against the fender of Shapiro's car. The metal object in his hand was a pair of pliers. Queenie was without defense and quickly succumbed to Rueben's attack. Rueben jammed the pliers between Queenie's legs and squeezed when its jaws found her body. Queenie cried out in agony, her body trying to slump, but Rueben never released his grip, pinching the jaws of the pliers with constant pressure until a shadow moved into view from the porch light.

"Let her go!" Tom yelled, his voice quivering but defiant.

Shapiro's head alertly jerked at the shrill of Tom's shout. "What the hell you going to do with that?" he demanded. "Don't tell me we have a hero here." Shapiro laughed.

Tom moved closer. In his hands, he held his father's Parker twelve-gauge, side-by-side shotgun. "Get away from her, I said."

Rueben released his grip. Queenie folded to the ground, bent over in pain, crying in exhausted whimpers. Shapiro reached inside his overcoat to find his pistol.

"Don't do it!" Tom screamed, thumbing one of the shotgun's hammers until it clicked, ready to fire.

Shapiro stopped the motion of his hand before it reached his pistol. "Easy, boy," said Rueben, who waited nervously for Shapiro's next move.

"Queenie!" Tom shouted. "Get in the house. Wake Father. Tell him to call the police."

Queenie rose slowly from the driveway; her cupped hand could feel blood beginning to soak through her nightgown where the plyers had ripped her skin.

"Do you think you'll stop me, ya tipesh? This ain't over, even if we leave. You can't watch over her forever," Shapiro shouted, keeping his hand near his pistol.

Tom reached for the second trigger of the shotgun and cocked it. Pointing its barrel at the fender of Shapiro's car, he squeezed one trigger, blasting a swath of buckshot into the car. The explosion resounded through the silent neighborhood, waking the sleeping residents, who began turning lights on. "I've got one more barrel, and I'll use it on one of you next. Which one of you wants to find out?" Tom said, his voice becoming more profound and confident.

Shapiro relaxed his hand, withdrew it from where it had been hovering over the pistol in his pocket. He backed cautiously to the driver's door, finding its handle to open it without looking. Rueben went for his door, grinning wildly, defiantly, knowing there would be more to come later to resolve the bold threats Tom Harrington had made.

Inquisitive neighbors stood on damp lawns rubbing the sleep from their eyes, wondering what calamity had befallen the Harringtons. With wondrous gazes, they watched the Duesenberg back out onto the street, its occupants paying no mind to their stares as

The Runners

it drove off in the early-morning light streaking slivers of sunshine through the background of trees.

Chapter Fifteen

Two sheriff's vehicles sat at the curb in front of the Harrington home, their red lights awhirl in circling swaths from their rooftops, slashing harsh, narrow beams of crimson across the early-morning neighborhood. The Smiths and the Hacketts, still wearing sleepwear, leaned from behind their half-opened doors, wondering what had happened across the street. Doctor Harrington finished attending to Queenie's injury and gave her a small dose of morphine to calm her. When the drug took hold, she quieted and slept. Tom sat in a chair near the front door, still holding the Parker shotgun, watching the street through the bay window. Doctor Harrington returned to the kitchen.

Helen Harrington perked a pot of coffee for Deputy Badder and Detective Beckham of the Oakland County Sheriff's office. They interviewed the Harringtons in the kitchen, wanting to know what would bring these men to Birmingham, to the Harringtons' house. The family spoke for an hour, telling the police how it all had come about.

Detective Beckham shaped his moustache with his left hand and tapped his pencil on his notepad as he said, "You have a significant problem, folks. I was a Detroit cop for ten years before I came here. I know these guys, and what they've been getting away with down in the city is enough to give a sane man nightmares. They are involved in just about every kind of crime you can imagine." Beckham drew a deep breath. "I'm afraid it isn't going away, either. That was no idle threat coming from Shapiro. He will be back. There isn't much we can do, other than keep a squad car with officers patrolling the neighborhood, but they know how to get around that."

The Harringtons felt doomed, smothered with despair and fear. "Do you have any idea what we should do in this situation?" asked Doctor Harrington. "There has to be something. This is my family we're discussing here. My children."

The detective nodded toward Tom, who was still standing guard. "Well, Tom has the right idea, but how long do you want to keep up that vigil? I know Shapiro uses a tommy gun that's capable of spraying the house with hundreds of rounds. That shotgun isn't going to stop them." Beckham wrote something down on his notepad. "Is there some place you folks can go, out of town, maybe…until things cool down some? If that's possible?"

Listening to the detective, Tom rose from his chair, and propped the Parker upright against its backrest. "Father, I could take her up to Shoepac. I know with Ike Powers and Ned Vermont around, she'd be safe there. Ike was a soldier in the war, you know. He could handle these guys."

"Shoepac?" Detective Beckham asked.

The doctor described the retreat and its remoteness to him, but added, "That's where this whole thing got started. Tom, I don't think we can ask Mr. Powers and Mr. Vermont to take on this kind of responsibility. That would put them in danger, too. These guys know about Shoepac. Might be the first place they'd look." He rung his hands in sandy swirls over the table for some time without anyone saying anything. Then he said, "But going there with Queenie might be our best option right now."

"Father, I know Ike would watch over us. That's just his nature," Tom said.

Beckham tapped his pencil against his notepad again, "That doesn't sound like a bad idea, Doctor. You say there are others who could help you, Tom? Would they be close enough in an emergency?"

"Yes. I believe Ike Powers might even stay with us; he's a remarkable man. There isn't much he doesn't know about survival. He was an elite soldier in France during the war. We suffered together once. I trust him with my life," Tom said.

"Maybe this isn't a bad idea, Doctor?" Deputy Badder said.

"I agree, Doctor," Beckham added. "How soon could you leave here?"

"We'll leave today, if the club is available," Doctor Harrington replied. "Helen, I'll call Vermont, and if it's available, be ready to leave as soon as you can. Tom, you, too. Pack that in the back seat." He said, nodding toward the Parker shotgun."

Helen and Tom saw the men to the door, thanking them for their time while Doctor Harrington placed a phone call to Ned Vermont that took only a few minutes to complete. He looked to Badder and Beckham, who remained by the front door waiting for the outcome of the call. He spoke as he walked toward them. "We're all set to use the lodge. He said we can have it for as long as we need it."

The neighbors departed from their lawns, returning inside their homes after the cops left, still imagining what had gone on, considering the silence that was now in the neighborhood that consoled them.

The Harringtons packed carefully but quickly, shouting out to each other what they would need to bring along. Helen wrote on a notepad everything Tom and the doctor said was necessary to bring with them.

Queenie was awake upstairs, listening, discovering with some trepidation that she would be taken to Shoepac Lake. Slowly, cautiously, she began to feel the comfort of hope and security. She sluggishly began to dress herself; even her slow, hesitant movements made her flinch from the pain of her injury, despite the waning numbing effect of the morphine.

The Runners

Before they left for Shoepac Lake, Doctor Harrington went to Beaumont Hospital to get more morphine for his daughter, resisting his feeling of guilt of betraying a doctor's Hippocratic oath to do no harm.

Chapter Sixteen

The family drove north under a colorless sky. The sun was buried behind rain clouds, like a candle glowing dimly under a bedsheet. Queenie sat nearly upright in the back seat, aching and hobbled with discomfort, a wounded bird unable to launch into a comfortable position.

By early evening they'd reached Rogers City. They drove past the melting remnants of snowdrifts, each mound leaching into the absorbing earth, and collected in lambent pools of water in the plowed fields outside of town. The pulse of Lake Huron thrashing at the shoreline came in consistent, measured waves. From Main Street, in the day's diminishing light, they could see it hurling in gushing spray against the piled boulders of the harbor's breakwall.

Emil Plath was about to flip the "open" sign over on the door of his market when Helen stepped from the car. Plath opened his door to let her inside. Doctor Harrington leaned across the seat to tell Helen he'd be right back, there was something he needed to do. Before Helen could speak, the doctor drove away.

"You made it by a nick, I'd say," Plath said, his white apron stained with blood from making sausage.

"Thank you for letting me in, sir. We're going to be up north for a while, and we haven't any food supplies yet."

Helen viewed the stocked shelves and cured sausages and hams hanging from steel hooks above the counter. Emil Plath removed the long sheet of wrapping paper covering the slabs of pork ribs, steaks, and whitefish fillets bedded on ice, all arranged neatly inside a long, windowed cooler. A short countertop with an ornate brass cash register showed finger-worn number keys, and a hand crank on its side made a crunching, metallic clatter when he cashed her out. Helen clutched the two paper bags against her chest like a set of young twins. Emil Plath helped by carrying a separate bag of meat and fish fillets that were packed with ice to the car. They spoke idly of the weather while waiting for Doctor Harrington, who was putting his car at the curb. He stored the groceries in the trunk. Plath spoke again of the weather in German, saying it was going to be, "*Beschissene Wetter*" for a few days.

The Harringtons drove through the piney forest road toward the cabin. The car swayed and rocked, like a ship riding on a rough sea, occasionally bottoming out in the wet ruts and rain-filled potholes. The vehicle's head lights sprayed the tops of jack pine trees in quick, errant beams as the car rolled up and over the gullets of the trail into the higher land.

When they reached the cabin, they found Ned Vermont's pickup already backed to the porch near the entry door. Gray spirals of fireplace smoke churned above the cabin's rooftop. It made for a calming sight after the long and uncomfortable journey. Ned and Ike Powers were unloading firewood Ike had split that morning. Some of it was still green but would burn if rationed on a good bed of coals. They had little time to prepare the cabin for its first visitors of the year. Ned and Ike watched as the Harringtons parked and stepped from the car. Tom helped Queenie from the back seat.

"Welcome, folks," Ned Vermont said, placing an armful of wood near the entry door, unaware of the dire events that had brought them there. Ike Powers nodded hello, his eyelids thinning when he smiled. Tom reached to shake his hand.

"You look older, Tom. I think you've become a man since I saw you last," Ike said at Tom's robust grip.

"I think it's time for that," Tom replied. "You remember Queenie, don't you, Ike?"

"Of course. Who could forget her and that voice." Ike regarded her but without commenting on her haggard appearance while she leaned weakly against Tom.

"Let's get her inside. I've got a pleasant fire stoked up she can warm to," Vermont said.

In the dusky dimness of the departing twilight, Doctor Harrington and Helen sat on Adirondack chairs below the porch overhang. Helen dragged on a cigarette; the doctor held an unlit cigar. A gasoline lantern, hanging on a hook, hissed a quivering flame above them, providing conversation light. Tom stood braced against the cabin log wall as he told Ike Powers and Ned Vermont of Shapiro's threats to Queenie's and the family. Queenie was sleeping inside on a bunk bed near the woodstove, acquiescing to another mild morphine injection.

As Tom spoke, the men listened without asking questions. When he finished his story, he added, "Ike, you had Shapiro figured out, but we were raised to believe in the best in folks. All Queenie wanted to do was sing. Queenie had no idea this guy was bad, and what he had in store for her."

Ike was quiet in his considerations. He rose from the porch railing where he had been leaning half seated. He flexed and rubbed the stiffness from his slow-to-heal wrist. "I know his kind, Tom. I saw men like him in harbor towns in France and England while I was stationed there. Con men of all colors. They got a good line because they've been practicing it a long time, preying on the vulnerable, the trusting folks who don't know the evil that's out there, mostly kids, like Queenie. It all sickens me."

Tom moved from the wall, fretting in short, circling steps around the porch. He stopped only to speak directly again to Ike Powers. "I hate to ask you this, Ike, but we need your help. When Shapiro finds out Queenie's gone…it won't take him long to figure out she's up here."

Doctor Harrington had been sitting silent, studying his uncut cigar while he listened, allowing Tom to make his case to the men, trusting the bond that had formed between them during their camping ordeal a year earlier. Finally, he cut the tip of his cigar and then leaned forward in his chair, bracing his elbows on his knees to light up. "I feel helpless," he said, drawing a short puff to get the cigar going. "I am humbled by this, asking for your help. It's my responsibility to protect my family. That's the minimum expectation of a good father. And yet when I became a physician, I took an oath to do no harm. Still, all this has stoked a rage in me I've never known. These men…" The doctor trailed off as he tapped his cigar, dispatching the fragile ash from its glowing end. "To hell with the oath."

Powers held his reply, contemplating what he could do to help them, what would be necessary to do. Tom returned to the wall, adding nothing, willing to wait as long as needed for the man to make up his mind.

"Doctor…Tom, I won't leave you alone out here. I can help." Ike turned to Ned Vermont. "I don't want you to stay, you've got Laura and the baby back home. You take care of them, okay?"

Vermont agreed, reluctantly.

Ike followed him to the truck. He took his pistol from behind the seat and a box of cartridges from the glove compartment and then returned to the porch.

Ned Vermont said he would check on them each day to cover any needs, and wished them luck.

The evening elements became silent and tame. The usual western wind had stilled, allowing the oak and pine trees to relax. The whisper of creatures prowling the night carried unimpeded throughout the quiet forest from afar. Over the hours, a glittering frost had formed on the windows of the car under the cloudless, star-filled sky.

Inside the cabin, a single lantern had been left burning, throttled down to a stunted flame. Everyone had selected their bunk and were bedded below woolen blankets, everyone except Ike Powers. Ike unhinged the twin doors of the woodstove to stoke the ash-laden coals back to life. His face brightened from the resurrected flames that began licking the fresh logs he'd placed inside.

Tom wasn't sleeping in his bunk that was close to the stove. He rolled toward Ike. Beside him stood the loaded Winchester shotgun he had removed from its hooks above the door. In a small voice, he asked, "I don't know what to expect, Ike. How do you think it's going to happen? Shapiro coming here, I mean?"

Ike peered into the flames as they waved and danced inside the stove, trying not to fall prey to a memory he wished to keep hidden. The flames of any fire brought back the time he'd sat watching a small fire with his platoon while the destructive glow of larger fires burned the small French village of Villedevant-Chaumont in the far distance. It was, November 11, 1918, Armistice Day. He winced at the memory of artillery batteries launching their ordnance toward the German positions near the town despite a treaty calling for the war to end. They were responding to German shelling that never ceased. He could hear their return volleys screaming overhead, some landing nearby, causing the earth and men to rise and fall from the sky in fragmented pieces. He remembered the unexpected silence that came after the crying and wailings of shattered soldiers had ceased. Ike flexed his shoulders and the taut and twisted scars bound across his back, recalling how the flame-throwers had bleached the night and scorched the earth as they sprayed their oily inferno into his platoon, engulfing him in flames. He hinged the stove gate levers together, shutting off the escaping firelight, sealing off his recollection of the war. "When they come, they'll come at night," he said. "Their kind always does."

Tom swiveled on the bunk to place his feet on the cool floor. "I was afraid you would say that."

"This guy, Shapiro, he's a gutter fighter. His kind don't fight fair. I'd expect him to come anytime, but the night will give him more advantage. Didn't he show up at your house during the night?"

"Yes, well, past midnight…when we were asleep."

"When you least expected it, right? When decent, hardworking people are sleeping," Ike said, rising from his knees at the stove. "Men like him disgust me." He flexed the blood back to his legs for a moment, and turned toward the cabin door. "Stay here, I'm going to take a look outside."

"Don't go far, Ike," Tom said, feeling anxious and unprotected.

"Try to get some sleep, Tom. I'll be close by."

Ike crossed the porch and stepped onto the crusty sand. His boots crunched past the layer of frost to settle on softer ground, leaving faint witness from the jagged pattern of his soles. He stopped and listened to what the night air held. His slow breathing puffed small clouds that dissipated quickly into the darkness. There was no wind to impede the sounds of the forest. He could hear forever, it seemed.

The cabin door scraped past its wooden threshold. Tom leaned out from behind it and whispered at Ike's thin outline where he was standing at the far reach of the mossy greensward. "Ike?"

Ike calmly motioned for Tom to join him. Tom was beside him within seconds, the Winchester mounted over his shoulder.

"Listen," Ike said once they were outside again.

This was how it was for Ike Powers and the Harringtons for the two days that followed. Ike would stand watch during the evenings, poised in the shadows on the cabin porch with his pistol wedged inside his belt, waiting for anything that would indicate Shapiro was coming. He slept on a bunk bed during the lazy hours of the afternoon, only to go back on his watch when the day's shadows stretched long before they blended into the night's darkness. The Harringtons played card games and long hours of chess, anything that would displace the ever-present fear and anticipation of Shapiro's arrival. The doctor intermittently tended to Queenie's injuries with fresh bandages and measured doses of morphine for her withdrawal cravings. Helen said she could see a glimmer of spark returning to her eyes, but the others knew she was only trying to encourage Queenie. They never ventured farther away than the cabin's outhouse on Ike's advice.

Tom began to follow Ike's sleep pattern and vigilant guard, joining him on the porch with the shotgun nearby. They discussed Ike's time in the military overseas during the war. Ike had never had the opportunity to go to college, so he asked Tom what it was like going to a prominent university.

"There's not much time to do anything other than study, if you want to stay there, but it's easy to get distracted by, you know, the after-class fun, then you fall behind," Tom said. There came a silence in the conversation. Resting his cold coffee cup on the porch railing, he tentatively asked Ike, "What was it like when you had to take a man's life? I think I need some advice, Ike."

Ike pondered Tom's question for a long moment before answering. "When I was a kid growing up here, my passion was to run. If folks saw me coming, they knew I was running. They'd ask me, why you always running, Ike Powers? I'd tell them, because I can, and it gets me to where I'm going with less distraction. It's no different for you, Tom. In a way, you're a runner, too. If you slowed down and fell to the distractions of those after-class temptations, you'd fail." Ike reached for Tom's shoulder and gripped it firmly. Tom felt his grip tighten uncomfortably. "When you're faced with danger, you have to decide if you are going to run: to it or from it. If you slow down, or pause, that will give your enemy a chance to run faster than you, and you know how that'll end up." Ike released Tom's shoulder. "You have to survive…but the act will stay with you forever. Some get over it, some don't. Me? I'm still running…" Tom rotated his arm to displace the pain from Ike's grip. Tom saw a side of Ike he never knew, and it frightened him. The man wouldn't hesitate to take the life of an enemy.

In the far-off distance, through the quiet forest, came a faint noise not produced by nature. The disturbance grabbed their attention immediately. Tom held his breath, shutting off the sound of his lungs, then exhaled slowly after he examined the evening. "I hear it… Is it coming toward us?"

"Go back in the cabin," Ike said, and repeated himself when Tom hesitated. "Go on, now. I'll be there soon." He didn't wait to see that Tom did as he was told and instead stepped off into the dense moonlit trees.

Tom returned to the cabin. Ike patrolled the darkest perimeter of the building, waiting like a soldier braced for battle. He heard the distant resonance of an undercarriage scraping and yawning as it passed along the road leading to the cabin. He knew the sound came from a few miles away, somewhere along the only road that led to the cabin. He knew it would take some time before a confrontation would happen, but he would be ready.

Ike waited a nerve-wrenching hour before he began his reconnaissance. He set out quietly into the shadowy forest, stopping frequently, bending at his knees, his eyes lowered to comb the frosted ground under the bright moon. There were several sets of fresh footprints leading away from the cabin toward Lake Francis. Ike became more concerned; whoever it was had similar stealth skills as he. He felt for his pistol and pulled it from behind his belt. He began following the footprints where they sunk into the crisp, mossy ground within the forest. The sound of his boots told he was stepping slowly, cautiously across the crust of the moss. Ike halted near a small opening that was lit more brightly. He crouched to the ground, inspecting the prints he was following. There he saw more footprints that revealed smooth soles joining the trail. Ike breathed deeply, expanding his rib cage gradually, as though the entering of air would give his position away by releasing his exhale. His breath clouded before him, like a resting train chugging steam at a siding. The rolling clack of a pistol's cylinder near his head made him halt.

"Don't move…" a dark voice said from close behind.

Chapter Seventeen

Tom peered through the cabin window, tapering his eyelids searching for Ike, but he wasn't in view. He could feel himself becoming nervous and fraught, thinking something must be going on, something wrong. His impatient worry got the best of him, and he tugged slowly at the door, trying to keep down the aching yawn the hinges made when it opened so as not to wake the others. He crossed the threshold of the porch to stand in the yard, listening. The moonlight shown on his face like a muted stage light, dropping a subdued shadow behind him. There was nothing coming from the forest, no trace of the vehicle on the trail he and Ike had heard earlier. They must be here by now, he figured, and as he stood there in the moonlight, he wondered if Shapiro or the other man who'd hurt his sister was looking at him, and what they might be thinking. Perhaps, he was in their gun sights.

Tom returned to the cabin quickly. There, he took a defensive position in a wicker chair in the center of the room facing the door, his shotgun resting across his lap. His mind raced with the possible scenarios he felt certain were to follow. Was he ready? Could he pull the trigger when he had to? He thought, too, of Ike's advice. He would act quickly when it came time.

Outside, gunfire erupted in echoing repetition from the stuttering but measured spurts of a tommy gun not far from the cabin, but not directed at it, either.

Off in the forest somewhere. Voices cried out in agonizing vulgarities. Tom felt compelled to rush outside to help Ike, but he resisted the urge because he knew that would leave his family unprotected.

    The calmness of the forest returned and there was no sound to give measure of what the results of the battle were. The doctor and Helen surrounded Queenie at her bunk, protectively clutching each other while Tom remained in his chair, his moist fingers lightly gripping the shotgun he now held pointed at the door. The stir of staggered footsteps across the porch ended at the cabin's door. They prayed for it to be Ike. The cabin door slowly hinged open. The outline of a bent man stood in the doorway, silhouetted by the bright moonlight. His soft voice spoke out, "How is everyone doing in here? You knew I'd come for you, Little Dove." Irving Shapiro stumbled inside, his tommy gun dangled from his right hand at his waist, like he was gripping an idle hammer. Blood leached down the sleeve of his left arm from what looked to be a slice from a sharp blade, dripping like a leaking faucet from his hand. Tom rose from his chair and pointed his shotgun at Shapiro's chest. When Tom squeezed the trigger, the hammer slapped against the dead primer. By the time he'd jerked the pump action to reload, Shapiro had lifted his machine gun and aimed it at Tom, firing a single round into his chest. Tom fell back against the chair, scooting it across the cabin floor. He crumpled against a bunk bed, panting for air.

Shapiro searched for Queenie through the dim cabin light until he found her wrapped between her parents atop her bunk. Doctor Harrington rose quickly to join Tom, but Shapiro waved his gun toward him, keeping the doctor in place. Queenie's pupils widened like an expanding flame on fragile cloth, sullied by Shapiro's assault on her brother.

Ike Powers rushed in the cabin and threw himself against Shapiro, wrestling him to the floor. He was bleeding from a bullet hole in his chest. He screamed to the Harringtons, "Take Queenie and Tom outside as fast as you can! Now!"

The doctor clutched his medical bag. He and Helen raced to follow Ike's instructions. Helen helped to lift Tom, and rushed to get Queenie, wrapping her in a wool blanket. They scurried past the combatants and into the cold evening where it had begun to snow.

Doctor Harrington began to treat Tom's chest injury, trying to determine how bad it was. Helen knelt beside them, holding Tom's hand. They didn't notice Queenie when she pawed through the medical bag, searching desperately for what she needed. She took a syringe and a full vial of morphine from the bag. They didn't see her enter the cabin, either.

Ike Powers was struggling to overcome Shapiro; he had lost a lot of blood and was becoming weak. Shapiro wasn't doing much better, but he was still able to rise to an upper position over Powers. His tommy gun was on the floor, and his hands were clasped around Powers's throat, strangling the life from him.

Queenie quietly moved in from behind. She held the syringe and vial toward the lantern light, filling the glass cylinder to its maximum. Queenie knew precisely where the carotid artery was on Shapiro's neck. She thrust the needle past his sweating skin and pushed the plunger forward until all of the liquid was dispensed.

Shapiro slowly released his grip on Powers when the over-dose of morphine began to set in. Queenie helped him roll on his back against the cabin floor, freeing Ike, who lay beside them recovering his breath.

In the dim lantern's light, Queenie crossed her legs to sit beside Shapiro, her eyes meeting his. Before he succumbed to final darkness, he said, "Sing it for me, Little Dove… Sing our song."

Queenie breathed a soft, melodic verse, "I'm a little lamb who's lost in the wood, I know I could always be good, to one who'll watch over me."

Chapter Eighteen

Snow clouds obscured the moonlight, making the forest dark again. The snow began to fall gently in tiny white parachutes, collecting and covering the bloodied ground where Helen and Queenie had dragged the body of Irving Shapiro from the cabin, leaving him there to be slowly shrouded by the heavy, wet flakes like a cotton sheet.

Tom was brought inside the cabin and placed near Ike Powers. Doctor Harrington attended to their injuries as best he could with his meager medical supplies. Queenie rested on her bunk bed near the stove, propped against a cabin wall. Helen cinched the wool blanket securely around her shoulders. She opened the stove doors to place some split oak logs on the ashen coals. The embers hissed and snapped at the green wood, laboring to engulf it into flames.

A gentle rap sounded against the cabin door, then it opened politely. Aandeg Boivin stood tall in the doorway, holding his single-barrel shotgun, its breech safely unhinged over the crook of his elbow. He held a machete in his other hand. Behind him on the porch were two Anishinaabe Indians and Skipper.

Boivin asked to enter the cabin. Ike Powers weakly lifted his head to say, "Doctor, these men came to help us. We owe them our lives."

The doctor nodded. Skipper followed Aandeg inside the cabin. "I wasn't sure you fellas would make it here in time. We are grateful for your help."

"We weren't going to leave you here to deal with Shapiro alone. Besides, we all have a good reason to …well, you know," Skipper said.

"Who are these people, Albert?" Helen asked. "Thank God they showed up when they did."

Skipper said, "I'm Skipper and this is Aandeg Boivin. I'll see that they get to a hospital right away." Aandeg nodded.

Skipper told the story of what Irving Shapiro had done, how he had tried to kill him, how he'd sunk his only love, the *Madame*, how he sprayed his Thompson machine gun into Aandeg's father, Chief Louie, killing him and his crew where they stood on the dock at Duck Bay. All over nothing but some watered-down whiskey. "That's why we're here, ma'am."

Doctor Harrington explained further. "When we arrived in Rogers City two days ago, and I dropped you off at Plath's, I went to find Sheriff McLennon to tell him that we were being pursued by Shapiro. He knew exactly who I was talking about, and that he had caused havoc with Skipper and the local Indians over on Drummond Island. McLennon said he would do what he could to intercept Shapiro if he had the chance."

"All I can say is news travels fast up here, Mrs. Harrington. Good or bad. There isn't much that doesn't get discovered when most folks are related to one another, say, even the sheriff," Skipper said.

Aandeg Boivin's Anishinaabe heritage began in ancient times, when three tribes of Anishinaabe met at Michilimackinac on the rocky shores where Lake Huron joined Lake Michigan. It became known as The Council of Three Fires. His father, Louie, had sat at the council as a tribal elder every year as the tribes continued their sessions over millennia. It was the Anishinaabe way to kill the enemy, to *nagaataan* for evil brought against its members. Aandeg came that night to stop the life of those who brought death to his father, the Anishinaabe Tribe.

Skipper offered to take Tom and Ike Powers to a Petoskey hospital in his sedan as early morning began. Doctor Harrington joined them, while Helen stayed with Queenie at the cabin.

When the sun rose, there was no sign of Shapiro, his men, or the Duesenberg.

On the far east side of Shoepac Lake, where a sand bluff rose high above a narrow beach, Irving Shapiro slouched dead against the steering wheel of his Duesenberg. Mo Rueben, with both of his hands severed and his skull split by Aandeg's machete, was sitting on the plush leather seat inside the car beside him. Aandeg Boivin and his two Anishinaabe brothers braced their shoulders to the rear fenders and pushed. The Duesenberg rolled over the precipice, crashing on the stiff beach, then tumbling forward into the bronze water, where it sank beyond the sharp drop-off into the endless depth of the lake. This was the place where bad Indians were buried.

Queenie and Helen sat on a bunk bed, waiting for Doctor Harrington to return from Petoskey. Helen brushed away the errant strands of hair covering Queenie's stare that never moved from a certain spot on the cabin floor.

Queenie changed her position, turning more toward her mother, resting her head on her mother's shoulder. She sat there only briefly, absorbing her mother's comfort, but becoming more restless and feeling pained by the craving that was gripping her. "How long do think it will take Father to get back here?" She fidgeted, shifting her position to where it was before. She minded the floor again.

"He should be back here before the end of the day, my guess," Helen said, tugging the blanket to cover Queenie's stomach, which hadn't yet begun showing the life growing inside her. "Stay put, and we'll talk some more about what's next." She looked about the cabin, the pooled blood that had stiffened with crusty edges drying on the cabin floor. "I've got to clean up this place before they get back."

Helen rose from the bunk bed to search for a bucket and mop then remembered they were stored in the outhouse. At the well head, she levered the long pump handle until it brought a cold stream of water filling the bucket. The muted gray sky had drawn away the remains of the night, bringing forth small birds that flicked and fluttered cautiously about the red-stained snow. Helen emptied the bucket over the blood, allowing the sand to soak it away. She filled the bucket again, intending to heat it on the woodstove. Before she went back into the cabin she lit a cigarette, shivering from the cold wind that sipped from Lake Francis to the west.

Alone, draped in the wool blanket, Queenie walked slowly toward the far side of the cabin to where she had been staring. Hidden below a wicker chair was a worn leather pouch, Shapiro's pouch that held heaven. She lowered herself to a single knee and picked it up. Upon spreading it open on the smooth wicker braids, it was all there. She folded it and held it at her side, then leaned against the window frame to gaze out on the new morning. Her free hand reached for her neckline, thinking of the pearls her grandmother had given her that she no longer possessed.

"Queenie?" her mother remarked when she noticed her through the breath-steamed window.

"Yes, Mother," Queenie answered, then joined her on the porch. Still holding the pouch, she pulled a cigarette from the pack sitting on the railing and held it limply between her lips. Helen's hand moved in with a lighter. The swirling smoke from their cigarettes joined the smoke of the woodstove and dissipated beyond the tree line. "What do you suppose we'll tell the police when they get here?"

Helen Harrington twisted the stub of her cigarette beneath her shoe. "Maybe the truth won't be so bad to tell. Maybe, they'll understand why you had to kill, you know, Shapiro."

Queenie dragged on her half-smoked cigarette and winced from the smoke that furled near her eyes. She tossed it toward the snow-covered greensward in an agitated motion. "What do you mean, 'maybe'? They had it coming, Mother. Maybe they won't find any bodies."

"Maybe they won't come at all. All we can do is wait."

Queenie tucked Shapiro's pouch beneath the wool blanket, as though she were guarding it. She began humming a dead song from her past. "I'm a little lamb who's lost in the woods…"

The End.

Christopher Chagnon-The Author.

Christopher Chagnon was born February 19, 1951, in Bad Axe, Michigan. Formerly the team photographer for the Detroit Tigers, and now a full-time writer, he has written three bestselling novels, *The Dregs of Presque Isle, The Ghosts of Presque Isle,* and *The Soldiers of Presque Isle;* the final installment of the *Chandlerville Chronicles* trilogy. He is an award-winning short story writer and photographer, living with Nannette, his wife of forty-five years, in Presque Isle County, near Onaway, Michigan. He manages time to hunt, fish, and play guitar or drums in a rock and roll band when he is not working on a new writing project.

Made in the USA
Columbia, SC
03 October 2018